MAD AS HELL

MAD AS HELL

M. NELSON CHUNDER

"A Master Tome of Revengemanship"

PALADIN PRESS
BOULDER, COLORADO

Mad As Hell
by M. Nelson Chunder
Copyright © 1984 by Paladin Press

ISBN 0-87364-295-3
Printed in the United States of America

Published by Paladin Press, a division of
Paladin Enterprises, Inc., P.O. Box 1307,
Boulder, Colorado 80306, USA.
(303) 443-7250

Direct inquiries and/or orders to the above address.

"We thank you for that which we're about to receive."

Contents

Warning:

Mad As Hell is intended for entertainment purposes only. Neither the author nor the publisher will assume responsibility for the use or misuse of any information contained in this book.

Introduction

It's grand to be back after hacking around Hoo Hoo Land (Latin America) for awhile. I'm all set to blow-dry the brains of uptight, ass-puckering, official America. So, beware bullies, bad guys, bureaucrats, pissants and others of the slimeball ilk.

My style hasn't changed; you can still cross-reference marks, tricks and gimmicks just by using the contents page as an index. But, for more fun, go to *Get Even, Up Yours!* and *I Hate You!* (Paladin Press), and see if you can combine some stunts for a maximum, mind-bending number on someone.

There is a purpose for this book, however. Despite what you may think about the lawyer-generated disclaimer *For Entertainment Purposes Only* that is plastered ubiquitously throughout this tome, I have written this book completely and totally to entertain you, gentle reader. My only purpose is to make you laugh.

Most of the characters portrayed in this book are fictional, as that's the only way many of them would have it. Any resemblance to real persons living or dead is a figment of your imagination. Likewise, many of the public utilities, government agencies and private companies depicted herein are mythical organizations. There are no dangerous additives, drugs or explosives, nor is the chosen occupation of many of this planet's people starvation. Never eat at a place called "Mom's" or play cards with someone named Doc. Plus, I love you, your check is in the mail, and I'd never come into your mind with an idea that was truly mean.

I can keep coming up with these disgusting books, however, only as long as you help me out with newer and more bizarre escalations of chicanery. Please send me your ideas, plans and scams in care of Paladin Press, P.O. Box 1307, Boulder, CO 80306. I answer each letter and card personally, so let me hear from you. Who knows, you may become infamous, too.

Finally, always keep smiling because that makes people wonder what, or whom, you've been up to!

M. Nelson Chunder
San Miguel, El Salvador

Additives

When it comes to paying back her enemies, Carla Savage doesn't horse around. Her unbridled enthusiasm for redoing nasties has earned her my friendship, as if that's not enough. Carla is greatly into the (ab)use of Di Methyl Sulf Oxide (DMSO). It's colorless, odorless, and it will penetrate the skin carrying with it any of a variety of substances you might wish to add. DMSO is easy to get in most areas of the country.

Carla's suggestions include mixing DMSO with antabuse if you want to choke up your alcoholic mark. Mix it with horse liniment. Mix it with the chemical of your choice and coat your mark's doorknob, steering wheel, etc. Perhaps some odorous chemical could be mixed with DMSO and your mark's favorite sexual lubricant.

Or, if your mark is a real worm, Filthy McNasty has a cure. Buy some relatively mild cat worming pills. Grind them up and put them into the mark's food. They cause nausea and a really classic case of the runs. A fine added touch for this moving additive is to impair the mark's use of the proper disposal facilities. You can lock the room, lock the stalls, glue down the lids, etc. Or if you can, simply interdict the mark in person by engaging him or her in important business or personal communication of a nature that makes it tough to break away quickly. Enjoy the mark's discomfort.

Speaking of great physics, you can add some real kick to a jerk's or jerkess's drink by including citrate of magnesia, which has a peppy lemon-lime taste as a wonderful disguise. In a heavy enough dose, it's a real bowel-buster.

Phenolpthalein ($C_{20}H_{14}O_4$) is a white crystalline substance used as the active ingredient in chocolate-based candy laxatives. To use it you must first dissolve it in ethyl (grain) alcohol. Once dissolved, it may be used as an additive in various foods and drinks. The advantage, according to James Q. Carter, is that you don't have to rely on the hoary old chocolate candy joke. He says it's great for getting back at rude and/or noisy partyholics.

Another of Carter's ruesome additives is neutral red, a water-soluble, crystalline, red dye which will go in one end of your mark and come out the other without causing serious harm enroute—with the exception of creating bright red urine. Because of its red color, you need to use it in disguised drinks, e.g., sloe gin.

It's been a long time since my old pal Neal Abogado has turned up in correspondence. Always a foot soldier in the pharmacological trenches, Senor Abogado has come up with a use of Medroxygprogestrone Acetate, a regulated, prescriptive drug. "It's a powerful drug that deadens the sex drive in a real Big League way," Neal writes. "It's so strong that Mr. Stud goes from 'canis lupus' to 'penis limpus' really quickly. It's great to slip this to some slime who's been porking the wrong lady."

During a recent talk show, Linda from Pittsburgh told me about a bad time she had at the tail end of a date with a would-be Lothario who tried to turn the backseat of his car into the Quickie Dickie Motel. Since she knew this was his standard MO with all the girls at work, Linda rigged his car the following week by spreading industrial strength itching powder all over the backseat, plus in and around the driver's side seat.

Killroy suggests that you purchase some large, pure-niacin vitamin tablets from your local drug store. Pulverize a couple of them and put them in your mark's food. About twenty minutes later, your mark will experience hot flashes, and his skin will actually turn bright red. This trick is totally harmless, says Killroy.

Butyric acid is not so harmless, and apparently it is becoming a favorite additive of active tricksters. Recently, I heard from Tyra Pierce, a Missouri student, who knows some good uses for this solution.

"I'm kind of small and young looking for my age, so I get picked on a lot," writes Tyra. "I found a fun thing to do to tormentors is to load a syringe with 15 units of butyric acid, then shoot the stinky stuff into their dorm room locks, car door locks or places where the marks will put their keys or hands. That way, the acid has a chance of traveling to other locales to spread your revenge even more. Think about toilet topics!"

Thanks to the kindness of an unknown Missouri pharmacist, plus some practice, Tyra now knows that sulphurated potash smells awful, is inexpensive and is a lot safer to use than butyric acid. It's great stuff and does all the same things that the more expensive and esoteric chemical accomplishes.

Mr. D. from Austin is another pharmacologic phreak. His contribution to our field of applied science is a chemical known as sodium silicate solution, available at almost any drug store for no more than two dollars a bottle. When splashed on glass, the liquid soon dries and becomes virtually impossible to scrape off. Needless to say, any car windshield treated to a bottle of this stuff is ruined, as he has discovered in field tests. Keep in mind that the solution dries to a clear appearance, so you'll want to add coloring to make it more overwhelming. Also think about adding metal shavings, shreds of paper, vomit, dirt, dog doo, food scraps, etc. to your concoction. The nice thing about this stuff is that you can put the liquid in plastic bags for easy throwing, so that you may not even have to leave your car to make a hit.

Then, there is muriatic acid. Killroy cautions that this stuff is dangerous, so wear goggles and gloves when you go to have fun. Buy some muriatic acid concentrate from a chemical supply house. You may have to sign for it in your state, so think ahead and decide whose name and ID you want to use. Use the acid to etch nasty messages about your mark in someone's cement sidewalk, wall, etc. It can also destroy car finishes and sensitive metal parts.

Airlines

I did a talk show in Ontario and found a delightful chap named N. J. Franchier. He had finally had it up to his rising gorge with the lack of service on some airlines and decided to *Get Even*. Here is his idea.

"I packed a zip-top packet of beef chunk soup mix with me in my carry-on luggage. When the time came for my stunt, I mixed some hot water with my soup. I quietly poured the soup into a throw-up bag, then pretended to be ill into the bag, making all the appropriate sounds. At the same time, my companion called the flight attendant.

"Just as the attendant was about to take my filled bag, I said, 'Wait a moment, please!' and offered the bag to my companion who dipped his fingers in, removed some chunks of meat and carrots and ate them. Before he helped himself to the tasty morsels in the bag, he politely offered some to the attendant and the others seated nearby who were incredulously witnessing this spectacle."

Now that is a great flight of fancy.

Animals

Since I've always felt that animals are generally nicer than people, I find it fun to make those furry friends my allies when it's necessary to turn a mark's property into Wild Kingdom. Carla Savage, a truly neat lady, has the following stunt in mind. She purchases liquid animal scents from companies that manufacture them for trappers, hunters, dog trainers and other users. It's that fourth category she likes.

"It sure is a drag for some dumb mark, especially if he or she is a fussy cat or dog owner, to have the old property overrun by lust-crazed coyotes, foxes and ferals, wildly seeking that elusive female in heat whose scent has been sprinkled all over the place by me. Of course, these wild animals are also very liberal when it comes to adding their own bouqets to the collection of markings," Carla writes.

This neat lady has more uses for the lab-produced scents, adding, "The concentrated scent stinks awfully. Imagine getting it on your clothes, especially if you are a jogger in a town full of dogs. You wonder what the awful odor is, but you'll soon forget that as you are going to feel like the Pied Piper of Puppydom. A very tiny bit of

scent will reach a dog's sensitive nose, even if it
doesn't reach the mark's."

Saucy Sybil also came up with a splendid and
unusual idea that uses a doggie to get even with
some rotten person in your life. Get a glossy
portrait-style photo of some truly ugly dog, put it
in a nice frame and write the inscription "To my
dear (add mark's name), with much love. Mother."
Then send it to the mark, or better yet, have it
delivered to the office.

Once again, and with accustomed literary
fanfare, we welcome back Stoney Dale, the ex-
professional wrestler who's as grand at chicanery
as he is at ringling. Stoney's lived all over the
country in his travels and had his share of nasty
neighbor dogs who crap on his lawn, chew the
garbage, scatter his papers all over the place and
yowl all night when some bitch is in heat. He
found a solution.

Buy one of those silent dog whistles, the kind
canines can hear, but humans cannot. Set your
alarm for 3 A.M. when your neighborhood dog
owners are asleep, go out and toot quietly away on
your new whistle. Soon, Stoney says, all the dogs
start up, lights go on and owners yell at their dogs
to settle down, ask what's wrong or call the police
to report prowlers because the dog is acting so
upset. Stoney says it works 100 percent well for
him.

This trickster also adds, "To get back at a dog
show sponsor, you might want to secrete yourself
away from the crowd and toot away on your
handy—and silent—whistle. Much to the dismay
of the owners, handlers and judges, these highly

trained dogs will run around in circles, bark, yap, cry and do everything but obey commands. It soon becomes a very comical mess," he relates.

Here is a nondamaging trick you can pull on a nasty dog. Normally, I am loath to suggest revenge on dogs, but this is a fun one. Bleaching peroxide will work on a dog's hair just as it does on human hair.

A number of people mentioned this one to me, but as I'd already seen *National Lampoon's Vacation,* I knew about it. You find a dead cat or dog—leave it to your imagination—and put a cutesy collar on it. Then, you attach one end of a leash to the collar and the other end to the bumper of your mark's car. Slide the corpse under the car. Hopefully, the mark will not spot the planted roadkill and will drag it all over town, or at least he'll drag it until an outraged officer of the law or vengeful citizen stops him one way or another. Actually doing this stunt is funnier than the film version.

Speaking of stench, I've described animal scents before, but skunk urine is the best, according to the experts, for smelling up a mark's property. Once the stuff is applied to a rug, car or clothes, you've provided nearly a year's worth of added nasal irritation to your mark's life. The experts say the best to use is natural, rather than synthetic, scent. See Sources.

Finally, don't rattle CW's cage out there in snowy Hastings, Nebraska, or he'll send you some rattlesnake eggs. Actually, they're the commercialized version of the old hooked-rubberband-and-washer-inside-the-envelope trick. Your mark

sees the envelope and thinks, "Rattlesnake eggs?"
He opens it, the band springs and the sound
scares the effluvia out of him. CW says this pre-
packaged version complete with printed label and
"warning" is available from Good Time Gifts,
P.O. Box 324C, Covent Station, NJ 07961.

Answering Machines

I'm not at all upset by answering machines. In fact, often it's fun to give a purposefully garbled response or to give your message by skipping key words as if the machine were broken. Q107 from Toronto will often hold a small radio or Walkman to the telephone and play some garbage to the machine. Or he will tape and play a selected portion of a radio station giveaway telephone call that makes it sound as if the answering machine's owner has won a contest, maybe.

Automobiles

Next time you're in a grocery store parking lot and you see your mark's flashy new expensive foreign car, try to visualize this. According to Austin's Mr. D, you can arouse the mark's paranoid ire simply by putting a note like this on his car:

Dear Sir,
I'm sorry for the damage I've done to your car. I will gladly help pay for repairs.

Sign the note with a second mark's name and phone number, then retreat to a safe observation point. You should soon see panic break out as the car owner returns to find the note. As he inspects his beloved vehicle, he'll undoubtedly find a few nicks and scratches he never noticed before, and he'll blame your other mark. He may demand restitution. Or if the owner finds no damage, he'll at least be left in a state of bewilderment, and you'll be left with the enjoyment of having pulled off a harmless practical joke.

Mr. D adds, "You can also run this against one mark by picking some really sharp auto at random or choosing a car belonging to some local

Mafia boss, politico, police chief or some other bigwig who will go after your mark."

As a practical joke, a drinking buddy removed and hid the distributor cap from Sweet Rita's car. She paid him back a month or so later when the gang was out drinking. "He had a whole bunch of drinks, was pretty blotto and of course, should not have been driving. But, he insisted. So, while the others delayed him, I did the world a favor and also paid him back, all at once.

"I ran outside and quickly spray-painted the inside of all his windows a flat black with quick-drying paint I had been carrying in my car for just the right occasion. He stumbled out to his car, got in and started it up. He sat there for three minutes, running his windshield wipers. Finally, after five minutes, he stumbled back out of his car screaming about going blind. One of us drove him home."

Doug Hummel of Berlin has a grand idea to immobilize your mark's car. He'd been reading security books, where he spotted a device called "The Immobilizer." It is an antitheft device that causes your car to stall out in about five minutes or so if it is not started properly, like with your key. Surely, says Doug, this same device could be installed on your mark's car, then the fail/safe switch broken.

If some big lug or nasty nut has wronged you, CW has a plan to immobilize him, too. According to CW's formula, loosen some of the lug nuts on the mark's car tires, apply some liquid steel on the bolt, then retighten the lug nuts. That's bad, CW writes, because eventually even a jerk like your mark is going to have to have that tire taken off the vehicle. Hopefully, it will be when he has a flat in a dark, deserted place in the worst weather you can imagine.

If you feel truly destructive, our veteran correspondent Killroy has an idea for using scissor and bumper jacks. He says that lifting the rear differential with a scissor jack will mess up the rear end of the vehicle mightily. A bumper jack can be used to buckle up parts in all sorts of places on today's modern car.

Clear-cast resin, available in most hobby stores, mixed with a catalyst (usually included), then poured on your mark's car, will create a very hard finish that is tough to remove, he adds.

In a different vein, Farmer Bill from Pittsburgh had some problems with government bureaucrats. When they persisted, he placed fresh manure around the fresh air intakes of their government cars. I guess a little fertilizer in deserves a little on the way out, too. It seems a fair exchange to me.

Finally, some gentle soul who declined to sign his or her name to a nice letter provides an amusing idea for the crumb in your life. Take several handsful of cookies or crackers and crumble them into tiny, birdfood-sized tidbits. Scatter them across the mark's unattended car. It's a sharing and exchange situation in which the little birdies eat the crumbs, then drop something in return on the mark's car. This is a good recycling venture, too, and quite efficient as it takes you about a minute to pull it off and about an hour for your mark to clean his vehicular dumping ground. Repeat as necessary.

Bakery

At one time, a bakery had dealt unfairly with our hero, so he decided to get a rise from them by costing them some dough. He obtained several dead frogs and froze them. Then, he took them to various stores which carried the mark-bakery's products. Ahhh, but let him describe it.

"I'd pull a loaf of French bread out from its bag, poke in a couple fingers and stuff in one of my frozen frogs, or maybe just half of one. I'd put the other half in another loaf. I carefully smoothed things back over and went on my way. But, then, it's all for entertainment purposes only."

I like this chap.

Banks

As Bartle Qinker points out, going through the bank's trash can be a revealing experience, as any garbologist will agree. He found bank employees' time cards, discarded loan applications and correspondence, and best of all, a complete set of microfiche cards with the names, account numbers and current balance of everyone in Alaska who banks with that particular institution.

"I had had a lot of trouble with this bank that was truly not my fault," Qinker writes. "So, I was thrilled to find one prize in the trash, a discarded direct-mail advertisement for a promotional gimmick. I checked some boxes on a pre-addressed card and ordered 250 promotional piggy banks for them."

Bars

A. H. Sylvester, who hails from Incarceration-ville, Colorado, is one funny lad. One of A. H.'s funnier brothers once had a beef with some bar owners because they'd fired him for no reason. He decided to fight fire with fire. He had a friend enter the bar with several vials of FFFG Black Powder which he used to load some of the explosive stuff in each of the bar's many ashtrays, mixed in with the butts and ashes. It made quite a fireworks show as folks in the bar unwittingly fused the booby traps with errant cigarettes. You can also bolster this type of action by adding some magnesium powder to the gunpowder.

Barbeques

Filthy McNasty suggests you add to the discomfort of your mark's next outdoor cookery by dumping a handful of powdered sulfur into the fire. If you also mix in ground red pepper, the guests will be reduced to tears as well as having their olfactory senses assaulted.

Bathrooms

Leave it to Carla Savage, the love of my pen life, to attack a person's toilet. As she points out, whenever a building is going up somewhere, there is always at least one of those portable outhouses for the workers. What a grand target! Carla notes that these Job Johnies are always isolated, portable, and made of lightweight fiberglass. They make great receptacles (a.k.a. targets) for fillers, additives, booby traps, animals, additions or just about anything that comes to your imagination. What a way to get back at a construction company, land owner or developer. Hit 'em where they, ahhh, well. . . .

This is so diabolical that I wish I had thought of it. Filthy McNasty wants to get back at an especially awful restaurant, although this gag would work anywhere, especially if the bathroom is somewhat dark. Take a store mannequin, put a noose around its neck and string it up so that some innocent patron or employee will stumble into the room and discover the body.

Once upon a summer, James Q. Carter was hassled by a nasty security guard during some much-needed vacation employment, i.e., the guard didn't like college kids. This plant featured black plastic throne seats in the employee restrooms, so old James Q. got some black roofing tar and coated the potty seat in the guard's room just before this runty rent-a-cop came off duty. As our hero was leaving the plant an hour later, he heard all sorts of horror-rumors about other guards having to use naptha to clean up a hysterical colleague. It seems some folks never do learn how to wipe up behind themselves, while others do quite well. Touche, James.

A chemical engineer to whom I told this story said that Prussian Blue High Spot Indicator is also great for coating your enemy's toilet seat. It is highly "contagious" stuff in that it will spread all over everything the infected mark comes in contact with. Think of the fun at home, with the family, the wash, etc.

Of course, you can also just simply put on a coat of fresh paint the original color of the seat and neglect to post a "Wet Paint" sign.

Want to wash your mark's might right out? Killroy once had a landlord who refused to get the leaky faucets fixed and refused Killroy permission to do his own work. Our hardy trickster stole into the landlord's place, unscrewed the aerator from several of his faucets, packed them with hard clay and put them back in. The man went nuts trying to figure out what had happened to his own water supply.

Beaches

The next time you go to the beach, Filthy McNasty says to take along about two hundred empty bottles and corks. When launched, each corked bottle should contain a neatly printed note that says something like this:

Scientist studying local ocean (or lake) currents will pay you $10 for the return of this form to him. Please indicate where you found this bottle and what time of day you found it. Your $10 reward will be forthcoming within the week. Just send this form to:
Full Name of Mark
Mark's Full Address

You can do the same stunt using helium-filled balloons, too. As a final twist, Filthy says to make it look like a promotional gimmick for a sci-fi-movie that's in town. The card will have little space ships printed on it, plus this message:

UFOs have landed! To hear the voice of a genuine Martian and get free tickets to (whatever), call (123) 555-1212, 24 hours a day.

The number you use, of course, will be that of your mark—hopefully, the home telephone. Getting calls like this at work could create some hassles with co-workers and the bosses.

Filthy also has a grand way of scaring the kapok out of obnoxious surfers and other beach bums who can ruin your surf 'n sun days. It's called "Shark Alert," and here's how Filthy works it: "I use a radio-controlled electric model boat with the top half (cabin and deck) removed. In its place is a large, realistic plastic replica of a shark's dorsal fin. The motor, receiver and battery section are sealed shut and waterproofed. The receiving antenna is folded along the fin and secured with epoxy.

"Wade out beyond the waves and send it on its way. Go back and find a secluded spot. With your transmitter, make it circle around the swimmers and surfers while controlling its movements. Your accomplice in the water will sound the alarm, shouting, 'Shark! Help!' and pointing to the deadly dorsal fin slicing through the water. While splashing and waving frantically, he'll scream, 'Swim for your lives!' "

Filthy then quickly guides the shark to a remote location down the beach to be recovered for use again.

Filthy adds, "With some stage blood and phony wound makeup, plus some accomplices to be 'victims' and 'first aid volunteers,' you can make a real production out of this stunt. You can really stick it to a resort area."

Bird Calls

Here's a nice musical duet for which we can thank Janie McGeary and Len Jenkins. You take a turkey, crow, duck or goose call into a sedate restaurant, church, funeral home, rest home or other highly inappropriate place to which you owe a nasty or two. Start calling from a place of concealment. Call and move out, call and move out. Don't overdo this one on the first mission, though. Come back again and do it again sometime soon.

Bitches

Saucy Sybil had a nice way of putting down a bitch and giving her disposition a well-deserved ride. As Saucy recalled her fun, "We had this particularly awful woman in our office, a real gossip and a mean, nasty bitch. Using a public messenger, I sent her a broom at the office with a note explaining that I wanted to be sure she was never without transportation.

"Everyone in the office knew about it, and she was never a threat to anyone again. She soon left that office, possibly riding the broom she so richly deserved."

Books

I bet someone in CW's family knew a frustrated librarian. Or perhaps, some jerk borrowed a book from him and never returned it. Anyway, here is a unique payback, courtesy of CW. Next time you're at the home of your mark (a.k.a. your book borrower), take along some glue and slip into his/her library. Glue some selected pages together in various volumes of the mark's books. Also, get your own books and secrete them outside.

Bureaucrats

Tor and Snow Dog are back again with some good, clean fun for entertainment purposes only. Have a bureaucrat who's screwed you? Does a dog have fleas?

This trick will take a little work, but it is worth it. You can't get a bureaucrat fired, but you sure can make her or his life difficult. Do some research and find out what law, bill or whatever provides the funding for the offending agency. The next time these chronic do-nothings turn a deaf ear to you, inform them in your most official manner that they might be interested in knowing that you have been circulating a petition to repeal the law that provides their funding. If you can sound convincing, and you have done your home-work, this really gets results. It's been tried with great success on agencies such as the Southern California Rapid Transit District. Of course, actually drawing up and circulating the petition can't hurt, either.

Another way to get to a bureaucrat is to file complaints against him. But file your complaints with other, related agencies. A dim-witted mail carrier, for example, might be reported to the Department of the Treasury for losing federal checks. Since the government keeps records of everything, this will be reported and might make things interesting if the victim tries for a promotion or transfer. Such complaints are also usually most effective if sent directly to the head of the particular agency.

Tor and Snow Dog also suggest putting your offending bureaucrat on the mailing lists of groups advocating the violent overthrow of the U.S. government. With the sociopathic paranoia of the Reaganistas, this is guaranteed to get success. They write, "You might give money in your bureaumark's name to one of these causes. Or at the appropriate religious or other national holiday, give his or her boss an inspirationally inscribed copy of something like *The Anarchist's Cookbook.*"

Finally, our cuddly California couple wants to know, have you ever asked to talk to someone with authority, only to be told that he is not in? The next time someone feeds you a line like that, casually ask who would be in charge in the event of a "disaster." If you get some lame answer instead of a name, why not "arrange" a disaster to see who or what crawls out of the woodwork?

The disasters can range from setting off the in-house fire alarm to placing an ad stating that tickets for a "secret" event (Rolling Stones concert, Frank Sinatra farewell appearance, giveaways of appliances) will be available at the location. Just happen to be around when the fertilizer hits the ventilator, and then go after the person who takes charge—mercilessly and unrelentingly. That's your head bureaumark.

One of the deadliest weapons in the bureaucrat's arsenal is the memo. I get copies of a lot of memoranda, but this one caught my attention because of its put-on potential. Just add a bit of devilish imagination, catch my drift, eh? Think forgery. Think imagined scandal. Think drugs. Think after-hours porno production parties. Think it, then memo it with copies to all, being sure to sign your favorite mark's name to the invention.

Ca Ca

If you're having neighbor problems, Mr. D from Austin says to take note of the times they leave their homes or cars unoccupied and unguarded. When you need to use a restroom and one of the neighbors is out of pocket, play "Santa Claus" by using his chimney as a toilet. Or leave "orphans" at his front door. Or perform the ultimate humiliation by taking a dump on the neighbor's car and sliding up and down the windshield to wipe.

Clothes Dryers

There's an even neater topping than pizza for your mark's dryer. Some hilarious reader with great measurements, signing the letter 177-38-1380, sent me the idea of spreading a half pound of Limburger between the barrel and the housing of the dryer unit. He says you can also toss in a dead squirrel for good measure.

Coin Boxes

Filthy McNasty wants to crowd coin boxes. When you board the bus, buy a paper or use a pay machine of any sort, make certain to bend the edges of your coins somewhat before insertion. The resultant grind of your crimped coins will make the machine's action sound like a couple of Ginger Baker rimshots and eventually jam the works. You can add some super glue if you like, much as a gourmet adds dressing to a salad.

Computers

A group signing themselves "Seniors Who Can't Spell" evidently know their computers well. They suggest that the addition of a small strip of magnetic tape to the little door that the disc goes into will screw the computer into a frenzy of nonfunctionability. Use black tape, they add.

They also report that the Radio Shack TRSDOS word-processing program Scripsit has a fun loophole. If you overload the memory with unnecessary material, it creates unprintable documents. This program keeps all blocks of words using the "Move" command in memory but does not record them in the usual place. An expert will have to come in to repair this mischief.

Tyra Pierce has been covering the collegiate scene for me and reports some fun things to be done with student versions of plastic lifelines to the computer commander—ID cards. If your school uses nonphoto ID cards with magnetic strips and is in any way lax with security, you have it made. Simply get your mark's student ID number, almost always a Social Security number, and pretend you are him or her. Go to the correct office, cry and moan about someone stealing "your" wallet with "your" ID card in it, pay

31

your five dollars and get a new card out and activated—all in the mark's name. At the same time, this process automatically destroys all verification of the old card—still securely in the possession of the unsuspecting mark. You can now do the whole bit on this person. You are that person in the computer's memory. And, best of all, as far as the computer is concerned, the mark, as represented by that old card, has ceased to exist.

In the same sense, this type of scam will work on the cards used in bank machines or department store credit departments. But as bank and store credit security is tight, you had better work on the card itself. Why not try to get hold of the mark's card long enough to use a bulk eraser to "clean" the magnetic strip, then return the card—all without the mark's knowledge. Hassle will be the order of the day when the mark tries to use this essentially blank piece of plastic.

Condoms

I wonder if anyone ever uses condoms for their historically primary function anymore? In any case, Alan from the North has a grand stomach-turner for us. Simply slip a condom over your mark's doorknob and coat it generously with a copious supply of Vaseline. Hopefully, you will do this so the mark discovers your trap at night or when the lights are out—an added touch you could take care of.

If you think I'm an evil degenerate, I thank you for your kind thoughts. But you ought to meet the Gripper. A graduate of the Hole-in-the-Rubber Academy of Everyone's Junior High School, he mixes super glue with alcohol, so the solution stays liquid until heat is applied. A small amount of this solution applied to a "lubricated" condom is a devastating experience. One smart lady loaded one up, so to speak, for a nasty guy who had done her wrong. It was their last act together, as he spent the next few days in the hospital. I like the Gripper and hope to hear from him again.

Credit Zap

According to Neal Abogado, who has a lot of experience in the business world, it is simple to get back at some scuzzball who's stuck you with unpaid bills or who has used his position to unjustly damage your credit standing or budget. According to Neal, it is fairly easy to infiltrate credit bureau operations in a small community.

"Use a fake name to rent a mail drop and open a phony checking account, complete with printed checks. Join your local credit bureau," Neal notes. "Then, using your phony business address/mail drop, run a credit check on your mark. It will cost you about ten bucks to do this. Pay for it with one of your checks and make sure your check doesn't bounce. Don't scam the bureau with bad paper.

"When you get the credit check printout of the mark, you will have the name, location and account numbers of many of his or her credit transactions. You can take it from there as a whole range of rotten things are open to your choice."

Please note that much of what was just presented may violate local, state and national laws. But then, what doesn't?

Dating Service

Call your mark's employer while your mark is not at work and ask to speak with him. The receptionist will explain that he is not in the office at the moment and ask if she can take a message. You then identify yourself as a representative of the local computer dating service and explain that he will not be able to use your computer dating service any longer until he pays his long overdue account. Obviously, this works best if you use the name of a real computer dating service in your area.

According to Killroy, you can embellish this scenario by altering the reasons why the mark is no longer welcome. Perhaps he did something awful, like peed or took a dump in a host's hot tub, joined some middle-aged ladies for a shower or streaked through a country club dining room wearing only a jockstrap—and that fastened over his head. Your only limit here is your imagination and the mark's employer's gullibility.

Diesel Engines

Our buddy Jimi the Z is also back from his hibernation with a fine tip for properly tuning your mark's diesel engine. Simply give the nuts holding the lines to the injectors a one-eighth twist to loosen them. Do it to all the engine's cylinders on one side only or to every other cylinder. Jimi says the idea is to start just a small leak. At 3,000 psi, this will make a hell of a mess on the engine, enough so that it might not start.

Drugs

A lot of people have written to tell me how great a high you can get with Yohimbine HC1, an active alkaloid found in yohimbine bark. According to others, it has excellent additional properties as well; the Crazy Chemist says it is a great aphrodisiac, as I reported earlier. I'm glad to spread the good word. You can buy Yohimbine HC1 from the Inner Center. But, as it is a sacrament of their church, you will have to become a member. See Sources.

Want to play "Pretend Pot?" It can be great fun if you want to involve parents, police, school authorities and other potential buffoons. When you burn dried strawberry leaves, they smell just like pot does in the smoking mode. RT with the dt's says to use your imagination with this one.

Let's get real again. Deanol is said to be a safe, natural stimulant that imparts a feeling of happiness. Its chemical name is dimethylamino-ethanol (DMAE). It is inexpensive and at this writing is readily available over-the-counter from chemical supply houses. Fencamfamine is a stimulant which is also available over-the-counter. It is medium priced and produces, I'm told, an effect somewhere between cocaine and speed.

Nature lover Annie Fellantori holds a Ph.D. in the study of psilocybin cubensis, or magic mushrooms, as our street friends know them. These delightful headbenders can be chopped into your mark's salad, which should soon Caesar on him. Knowing better, you can take them recreationally.

So much for fun. Let's get nasty. South American Indians can't be too far wrong, especially when they make such good poisons. Dieffenbachia, or "Dumb Cane," is a very popular decorative plant often found in hotel lobbies and larger homes. It is also popular with the Indians, who use the plant's extract to poison their spear and arrow tips. A bit of the poisonous, milky liquid on a person's tongue renders him mute for a period of time—thus the name "Dumb Cane." All this from those folks who gave us curare.

According to Filthy McNasty, Lobelia herb may be bought at most natural food shops. Added to food, it will cause the mark to toss it all up. Or if you want to send your mark on a long trip, grind up and sprinkle some Heavenly Blue morning glory seeds on his food.

Then there is the hard logic of a contributor known only as Cold Steel, who sounds to me like a nurse. Cold Steel writes, "Hospitals use narcotics, it's a fact of life, right? Every drop of every controlled drug must be strictly accounted for, and this fact gives the seasoned trickster another target. Simply tip off the local narcs that a drug ring is operating from your favorite hospital. They *will* investigate."

On talk shows and in the mail, I get a lot of complaints about the super-sniffer dogs the narcs use these days to hassle righteous folks about drugs. Uncle Bill Basque has a solution. First, these dogs have very sensitive noses. Second, with the proper materials, you can render their sensitive noses useless for days, all without really harming the dog.

For example, while eating his hashbrowns in Dallas one evening, Bill told me that ammonia and bleach powders or smelling salts spread on the floor where the animals will be working wipes their sniffers right out.

Drunks

If you've ever suffered through drunken captivity in the military, college or hunting camps, you'll appreciate Tyra Pierce's fine revenge. This is for every guy who's had to endure late nights and early mornings with a troupe of untrained amateur drunks doing their things.

Buy a few cans of cream of something soup—it doesn't matter which. Set them in the hot sun for a few days until the contents cook ripe. Do the same with two cans of beer. Mix the two together and put them both back in the sun for some additional curing time—maybe a day or two. Don't smell this vile mix, just bottle it, cork it and set it aside until your drunken companions or neighbors do their next thing.

When the louts eventually settle down, here's what you can do with the mixture. But let Tyra tell what he did, "I snuck into their room after passout time and poured this mixture over the toilet and the bathroom floor. Then I left, dripping the rest out into the room toward some beds. I quietly closed and locked their door from the inside as I left the area. When they stumbled around later in the morning and found the mess, they naturally assumed it was one of their own. It started a small civil war."

Explosives and Bombs

Steve Tedeschi sends me the formula for what he claims is he loudest M-80 possible. He notes that his research turned up the formulae and methods that the fireworks industry used years ago when they made the old-fashioned M-80s. He also claims these are more stable and less prone to decomposition than other formula M-80s. That means it's safer to save these for a rainy day trick, I guess. Here's Steve's formula:

Potassium Perchlorate	50%
Antimony Trisulfide	25%
German Dark Pyro Aluminum	25%

You load the mixture in a standard-sized fireworks container, approximately 1½" by ⅝", and seal with proper end caps and fusing. Steve writes that in his fifteen years of making fireworks, this is the loudest he's heard of the hundreds of combinations and compositions. He also notes it has 100 percent reliable ignition with cannon fuse.

Going from the chemical to the comical, we run across the Indiana Cave Man, who wants you to meet a dead rat in an explosive context. He tells how to make a "Dead Rat Slop Bomb."

Stuff a dead rat, pet or other small varmint into a glass jar, add two inches of water, screw the lid on *tightly,* hide it behind the mark's sofa or in another appropriate location. Decaying organic matter releases awful gas which will explode the bottle after a few days. Delay time depends on temperature and initial conditions. This slop bomb has the advantages of high potency and long delay. It's especially effective if it contains the mark's pet or portion thereof, as lots of potential exists here for making it look like the mark's kids did it. Pint or quart mayonnaise jars are ideal.

Unknown to all but a few of the world's population, Hastings, Nebraska, is the home of *Shotgun News,* a grand wishbook for gun collectors. It's also the home base for CW, who is still running free and has some new ideas.

"One of the worst things I know is my truly awful stink bomb mixture," our bombastic chemist writes. "Take a quart jar with a rubber seal. Add a quarter inch of crystal Drano. Add one or two inches of water. Let it sit in a warm room for about an hour to allow the gases to cook with the lid on. Let the gases cool, then open the lid and add six egg whites—only the whites. Add a quarter cup of Methylene Blue, then fill the jar to about an inch of the top with water and seal it. Let it sit for four to six weeks.

"You use this bomb by shaking the container really well, then placing it where you wish. You can pour it (be careful of splashback), throw it, open it or leave it sit until the action wrecks the rubber seal and lets the odor seep out. Devastating," notes CW.

Then, there is the Masked Revenger, who surely does have a deep well of patience. For nearly a year, he put up with some college-dorm bozos who stole from him, got sick on his clothing and insulted him by just being there. When he did *Get Even,* he did so with a bang.

"I'm sensitive enough not to inflict personal injury, so I guess this falls into the calcium carbide class. But here goes," he writes. "Purchase a can of calcium carbide, a bottle cork, a disposable syringe, a small amount of hydrogen peroxide, a length of bell wire, a long, skinny balloon, then find a high voltage/low amperage power source, such as an electric fence transformer.

"Punch two holes in the cork and insert two pieces of stiff wire in the holes, leaving enough for leads on one side of the cork and just enough for a spark gap on the other. Epoxy all these so there are no air leaks.

"Inflate and deflate the balloon several times to stretch out the rubber. Powder a couple grains of carbide and put it into the balloon. Be very certain the inside of the balloon is totally dry, then slip the end of the balloon over the cork and clamp it securely with a plastic tie.

"Wait until the middle of the night when the mark is totally asleep. Stick the balloon under his/her door as far as it will go. Then push the syringe through the cork and fill the balloon with the hydrogen peroxide. This will combine with the calcium carbide to provide *fun* gas and leave enough good old O^2 to ensure ignition.

"Clip the power supply wires to the wire leads coming out of the cork, and as the balloon inflates all the way, simply complete the electrical connection. If the *Barrrooooommmmm* shock doesn't knock you senseless, take your power supply with you and run like hell."

According to the Masked Revenger, in his initial tests in a closed, empty dorm room, the device shook rooms two doors away. In actual use, it also leaves very little physical evidence as most of the contents are destroyed. It does leave behind a very strong odor.

Fuses

So you have loud, unruly neighbors who play the stereo too loud and long. Or you live next to a garage band that practices during the hours when Dracula stalks. Filthy McNasty will help you. Use super glue to disable their fuse box. Or turn off their power and quickly padlock the fuse box shut.

Another fusionary idea was shot from the brain of Bullet Bill. He likes to raid his mark's box of spare fuses, putting clear nail polish or clear paint on the electrical contacts. Bullet's other idea involved a photo. He writes, "I taped a picture of a dynamite stick to my mark's fuse box, along with a note which read 'Next time, I put explosives in here and when the lights go out in the house and you open this box, your lights go out too. BOOM!' It was great, according to his sister who was my accomplice."

Garden Hoses

Does your mark take terrific pride in his garden? If so, back pour some weedkiller or defoliant into his water hose and replace the nozzle. Also, threadlock is wonderful stuff, as water, oil, gasoline and many solvents will not touch it. There are many suggestions for using this product, including garden hoses/spigot hook-ups, home/apartment plumbing appliances and installations.

Killroy says that it's great fun to run your mark's garden hose into a nearby tree and afix the nozzle to a branch pointed at the faucet valve. He has done this many times, and it always proves to be very irritating to your mark when he goes to turn on the faucet.

Goldfish

Little Billy Gondorrhea once needed to get back at a nasty friend who killed his pet rock. Billy put some Jello mix in the mark's goldfish bowl. Another fishy stunt was pulled by Bullets Morepage, who got some freshly deceased goldfish free from a pet store. She made them into a disguised sandwich for her mark and smuggled it into his packed lunch. Another bullet was fired in the name of revenge.

Graffiti

As before, I present some samplings of useful graffiti I have seen as I travel this grand land of theirs. Perhaps you can use one as is or modify any or all for your own uses. These make fine postcards, buttons or bumper stickers.

DON'T BLAME ME, I VOTED FOR HITLER
I BRAKE FOR JAYNE MANSFIELD'S
   HEAD
I CAN'T DRIVE ANY FASTER, HALF MY
   ENGINE BLOCK IS JIMMY HOFFA
I'M NOT AS THINK AS YOU STONED I AM
YOU'RE NOT THE FIRST BUT YOU CAN
   BE NEXT
ARE YOU STONED OR JUST STUPID
I'M NOT EASY BUT I'M OPEN FOR
   DISCUSSION
SIT ON A HAPPY FACE—MINE
TO GET REALLY STONED, DRINK WET
   CEMENT
DROP YOUR PANTS, I THINK WE'VE
   MET BEFORE

Greeting Cards

Finding fame in Madison Avenue's advertising industry is the sort of ambivalent feeling a dehydrated person gets when he finds a bucket of warm spit in the desert. But, that's not how I felt when I discovered that two young advertising executives, Barbara Davilman and Nina Tassler, had commercialized my *Get Even* concept with their own business venture called Bittersweet, Inc. The moonlighting ladies came up with nasty "greeting" cards for the same sorts of rounders I go after in my books.

My favorite of their cards shows a cute young couple, obviously nude, standing coyly behind some bushes. The headline reads, "Do you remember that wonderful time when. . . ?" Then, the kicker comes on the inside panel, "Oh, never mind. That wasn't you." Great! I don't have their address, but the card line is Bittersweet, Inc., in New York.

Grenades

Nothing new and different here, as anyone who can read an army manual on making his own weapons can figure this one out. Suppose you really want to trash the inside of someone's apartment or automobile. Take an M80, cover it with auto body putty or epoxy, then dip it into a dish of BBs. The result is a truly effective fragmentation grenade. Thanks, and a tip of the hat over toward the Right in the direction of Ed Sasquatch.

A safer and more fun grenade update comes to us from Killroy. To make a first-rate paint grenade, go to your local hobby shop and purchase some Clearcast resin ball molds. They are *very* thin glass, inexpensive and shaped like miniature vases. They come in various sizes and can be filled with paint, then corked or sealed. You do the rest.

Hitchhikers

Ever since one of them deliberately vomited a ripe pizza in his car, Ray Domino has hated hitchhikers. He was also robbed by a hitchhiker of a gold pig head, a family heirloom he had on a necklace. "The bastard took my wallet, too, but I really missed the pig's charm."

So Ray now goes out of his way to bother abusive hitchhikers. He carries an arsenal of antihitchhiker ordnance in his battered old VW, including water and paint bombs, shaving cream pies and bags filled with itching powders and other irritants.

"In my other car I am building an auxiliary windshield wiper reservoir and hose to be aimed horizontally off the bumper so I can drive slowly by and strafe them with whatever mixture I choose to include in my reservoir."

If I were you, I'd stay out of Ray's way on the open road.

Hookah

I put this one in to educate all you druggies who know only the crude slang term "bong," when what you really mean is a hookah—the true name for that delightful smoking device. On the other hand, maybe you're from New England and thought I meant something else. Nonetheless, the Sonic Boomer has this really fab idea for a bong bomb.

"This doper had done something really bad to some really nice people and some corrective behavior was in order," says the Boomer. "I added some methyl alcohol to his bong instead of the customary water. Flooosh, it was meltdown time."

He added with his hearty, humanitarian laugh, "Nobody got physically burned, but I suspect he had to change his shorts after the flash went off."

Hospitals

Most hospitals give newly admitted patients an informative brochure, folder or packet of materials outlining such subjects as visiting hours, treatment procedures, mealtimes, etc. According to Cold Steel, our in-hospital spy, an enterprising trickster could add some new items to these patient packets. One item could be a real or bogus business card for an attorney whose specialty is medical malpractice; nothing freaks out a hospital administration more than the thought of a lawsuit. It will tighten their pucker factor a hundredfold. You could also include information on drug connections inside the hospital, how to have sex with nurses, interns, custodians, etc. Or advertise an in-house hooker/gigolo service. Use your imagination.

A few words of caution, though. Hospitals, even bad ones, are in the business of patient care. You must never, ever, do anything that will put any patient in jeopardy in any way for even a moment. *You* might end up in old St. Wimpus some time. So, be careful there!

Houses

A grand cop turned writer, Joseph Wambaugh, once shared a talk show with me. He told me a true story about a true prick of a precinct captain whom nobody liked. When the jerk and his wife went on a two-week vacation, some jokesters advertised his house at a very low price and actually had it sold before the owners returned. It created one hell of a fiasco that eventually reached city hall.

Speaking of homes, once a builder screwed Killroy over, not a smart move! Killroy poured a bunch of used motor oil over the drywall in the mark's new construction job, making it impossible to paint over. It added up to costly replacement time. Or to paraphrase the Archduke of Kissinger, one man's vandal is another man's freedom fighter.

Insurance Companies

If your mark works for one of the uptight companies in the insurance industry, Jimi the Z says you're in luck. From experience, he knows that most of these ripoff corporations automatically discipline or terminate employees who make any sort of public dissent or uproar with the legislative or regulatory bodies that deal with the insurance industry. Thus, you could have your mark supposedly write a nasty letter to the editor of a newspaper or magazine, a complaint letter to a regulatory agency, a kudo letter to the Consumer Advocate in your state, or have the mark quoted in a newspaper- or magazine-piece critical of the insurance industry. The fun and nasty games of mistaken identification and paranoid charges and countercharges will give you many guffaws. You can work this same one in the banking industry and the military as well.

Jammers

Exercising his reader's rights, the Stainless Steel Rat is back with his version of a simple, homemade "fuzzbuster," an FM signal jammer. You'll see his diagram following these instructions. The specs include an output of 50 to 900 MHz, using 9 to 16 volts and drawing 5 ma.

Barney Vincelette has to be one of our more delightful tricksters. A veteran of the *Real People* TV show, this guy lives in a house coated with luminous paint and illuminated with black light. He lived in more conventional apartments, but he got upset with people running loud TVs and stereos at uncivilized times of day. That's when he designed and built jammers which work well. Here are his diagrams, with his welcome to help yourself.

There are a few jammers available commercially too. (See Sources.) A fun guy I know bought one from Johnson Smith and used it to block out a period of closed circuit instruction in the company he worked for. He simply carried it into the meeting room in his briefcase. In another instance, our old pals, Some Very Funny Seniors, spirited one in the false ceiling of their school auditorium, disrupting a planned TV show that would have gotten some very lazy teachers out of the classroom for a few hours.

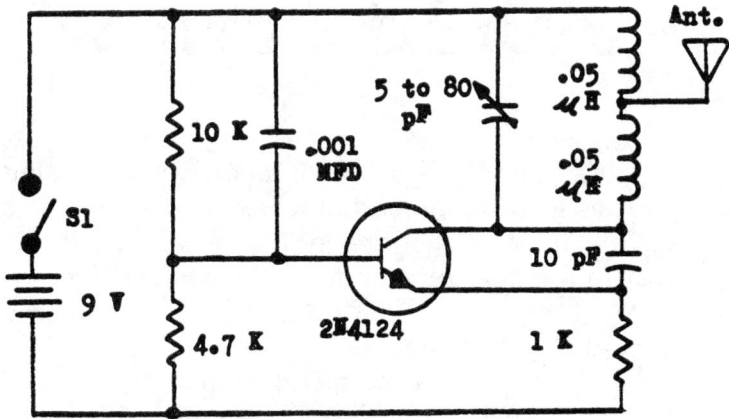

The Stainless "Steal" Rat

Job Interview

It's a simple, basic bit of monkey warfare, but as President Reagan has showed us so often, all is unfair in war, politics or American business. Here's a neat thing to do to the competition, according to Annie Fellantori, who actually is a straighto potato herself.

"If your mark is going on a job interview, call the place he's interviewing and cancel the interview. Or move it back, making the interview time earlier by two hours. That way, the mark shows up late," Annie says with a hard, evil look that could open a clamshell at a hundred yards.

Keys

Another of Mr. D.'s harassment techniques is far-fetched but worth a try if you're bored with the usual. Due to the possibility that this might prove a little risky for your target, he suggests that you be more careful than may seem necessary. Here's the trick. Collect various keys, particularly house keys, and place them on key rings. Tag each ring with a label showing your target's name, address, etc. You might also list a high-dollar occupation, such as gun collector, jewelry connoisseur or diamond specialist. The tags should be roughed up to look worn from use, and the keys should be slightly tarnished, rather than suspiciously shiny and new.

Judiciously deposit the tagged keys in a number of locations around the scuzzbag areas of town. The idea is to entice interlopers to visit your target's home and possibly try to break in. The chances of such luck are nil, but even if honest citizens contact your target upon finding the keys, all is not lost. You will have placed your target in the unpleasant position of wondering what the hell is going on.

Labels

Many tricksters now use the Dymo Label Maker to create anonymous messages for their marks. As James Q. Carter writes, "It's a lot easier than cutting letters and words out of newspapers and pasting them on paper." Carter also uses his homemade labels for mark's store windows, walls and display areas, issuing such consumer warnings as Rip Off Artist, Price Gouger, Sodomist, Thief, Pervert, Inept or whatever he thinks describes the mark. He also knew someone who sent a message to his mark using a label maker to create a tape reading "B-O-O-M! This could have been a letter bomb." Oh, and don't forget to wipe your prints off the plastic tape, he adds.

In a like sense, the Indiana Cave Man suggests that doing your own silk-screen printing is easy and inexpensive. Print some large official-looking, adhesive labels, something to the effect as follows:

CRIMINAL EVIDENCE
Impounded by the
FEDERAL BUREAU OF INVESTIGATION
TAMPERING WITH EVIDENCE IS A FELONY
Maximum penalty $10,000/5 years imprisonment

for disturbing this seal without permission of
FEDERAL PROSECUTOR'S OFFICE.
(add appropriate long-distance phone number.)

Use these stickers to seal the doors, trunk and
hood of the mark's car. Another variation: Seal
the mark's house or business while he's on vacation. Use *really sticky,* thin, paper, bumper-sticker
material, so the mark will have more trouble on
his hands when he finally gets around to remov-
ing the labels.

Landlords

Once upon a terrible time, a leaky landlord troubled our Captain Kill. The Captain is a veteran trickster, so he took his trusty roadkill patrol out on a specimen hunt just before final inspection to vacate the premises.

"The guy was a real jerk, and I wanted to get back at him a few days after I had cleared the state with my deposit refund cash in hand. I found the perfect resting spot for that roadkill.

"I took the grate off the heat register in the apartment and pushed the dead 'possum back as far as it would go. Then, I replaced the grill. An hour later I had my refund and was gone. It was winter and the heat ran a lot. I suspect my ex-landlord got quite a surprise a couple of days later when he showed the place to the new tenant. The place was a rat trap when I lived there, so I turned it into a odor trap when I left."

Lawns

Colorado's Bill Basque is a great friend, but a badass if you're his enemy. He likes to lay lengths of thin wire in his mark's lawn so that when mowing occurs, the wire may bind up the mower. Or if the wire's very thin, it will rip and fly off like shrapnel, scarring the mower blade and the mark. If it is too thick to cut and binds the blades, hopefully it will also burn out the motor.

I'm sure you've all seen the wonderful ceramic statues that adorn the lawns of many mold-minded middle Americans in towns like Polyester, Ohio. Why not create a formerly living version of the same for your mark's lawn? The idea here is to help with the landscaping some evening or while the mark is away for a period of time by propping up large roadkill in the mark's lawn. Dead deer, dogs, even groundhogs will work well, especially if rigor mortis has already set in.

Linoleum Floors

Have a mark whose place is furnished in classic lino? Pour a bit of methyl ethyl ketone (MEK) on the floor—instant destruction. According to Killroy, the stuff will also scar and craze plexiglass.

Lockers

Once a bitchy little preppyette made life nasty for our Masked Revenger. It had to do with high school lockers. So he made two trips to the school office: One was to boost a couple memo sheets, while the later visit was to place a forged order to change the lock on the girl's locker in the custodian's box. You can imagine the fun—unofficial and later, official.

Mail

If your mark has a rural mail box, go over at night and remove the entire box. Leave a printed, official-looking notice on the support or on the house door that reads something like:

> Your mail box has been removed by order of the Postmaster General because of failure to comply with Federal Regulation 86R-#1, subparagraph F-785-GH. Contact your local Postmaster for further instructions.

Do this after the mail has been delivered on a Saturday. The phone calls the mark makes will be wonderful, as will the confusion at the post office. For this special delivery item, we owe a parcel of thanks to David Kirkpatrick.

As reported before, for years I have either routinely tossed out junk mail or returned the postage-paid envelopes affixed to a package of heavy rocks. You can also gross out selected junk mailers by returning the envelopes stuffed with hardcore porno pictures. James Q. Carter takes it one step further. He learns the name of the company's CEO, then sends the porno addressed to the boss's executive secretary.

Bartle Qinker has a softer approach. If Company A sends him twenty pages of promotional literature and/or catalogs selling its stuff, while Company B is insisting he join its Junk of the Month Club for the eighth time in four weeks, he simply crams all of Company A's mess into Company B's postage-paid return envelope and vice versa, then mails it all back. Qinker adds, "I leave my own name/address sticker on all items so they know who loves them, the bastards!"

Tor and Snow Dog tell me that you can use a computer to generate multiple mailing list entries for your mark. Let's say the mark's name is Ronald Wilson Raygun, 1600 Pennsylvania Avenue, Washington, DC 20500. You can enter separate entries for R. W. Raygun, R. Wilson Raygun, Ronald W. Raygun, Ron Raygun, or any number of variations and spellings. Then start with some very slight variations in address, to add dozens of mailers to the same mark. It might also be fun to send a lot of the mark's junk mail to neighbors.

Far from burying his head in the sand, R. P. Ork, our favorite baiter of "them filthy, godless commies," is back with some malevolent mail maneuvers. Ork says he's tired of being on left wing, liberal mailing lists, and as he can't personally shoot all these unpatriots, he uses their postage-paid return envelopes to get back at them.

"All of these mail bank outfits use automatic letter openers on an assembly basis. So I put a little sand into each envelope before sealing it, and I mail it back to them. The machine slits it, and the sand dumps out into the machine. Stop the presses!" Ork says it works everytime.

Managers

RT is an extreme example of the Peter Principle gone berserk. Actually, he is a high-management type in a large institution which has several branch offices around the region in which the company operates. He is also a hardcore jerk, a man who gives Kafka-like meaning to the term incompetence. You could count his friends on one hand and still have four fingers and a thumb left over. Get the picture?

Because he was exceptionally nasty and snotty to his subordinates, they chose to get back at him. They targeted his office because the man was a victim of executive trappings. As RT's old nemesis, the IFC Poster Child, tells it, "If the man had half a brain, we'd have immediately driven him bonkers. As it was, we had to work harder."

For starters, they doctored the photos in his office for several weeks, e.g., slipping new photos in the existing frames. On his own wall-mounted portrait (yeah, he had that in his own office), they burned out the eyes. Then they pasted a fake moustache on the new print he had mounted.

After a month, he ranted and raved to both his staff and to security about this office vandalism. The breaking point came when someone put a bunch of helium-filled condoms in his small ad-

joining conference room just prior to his march-
ing in a group of important clients for a meeting.

As a finale, the revenge seekers waited until
he left for a three-day conference. Then with the
help of a forged work order and a couple of co-
operative maintenance workers, they had his
entire office moved to a branch plant forty-five
miles away. RT returned to a bare office. All the
staff feigned total ignorance, showing him the
work order with his own perfectly forged signa-
ture on it. It took him the entire day just to locate
his office contents and ten more days to get the
move straightened out. He got no sympathy from
his fellow executives. It was wonderful, and
according to Poster Child, the campaign contin-
ues. He adds, "Going to work is fun again."

Mass Transit

Filthy McNasty has been to the pet shop and bought several populations of ant farms. Filthy's ant farming is more than a hobby; it's shared with the public.

"I'm going to populate my least favorite bus with thousands of the little critters. Scratch, scratch," chortles Filthy, with no picnic in mind.

Sometimes Filthy takes a whoopee cushion on board the bus or trolley, adding, "I drop some calcium carbide on the floor, then sit on this cushion. The combination really moves people."

Here's another. You get on a bus or jitney carrying a small, closed, cottage cheese container with some fork holes punched in the lid. Hopefully, it's on a nonstop freeway line. You suddenly yell, "Oh shit!!" Wait the few seconds while all attention swings and focuses on you, then look back at your fellow travelers and say with controlled-panic gravity, "Dear God, all of my Brown Recluse Spiders got loose on this bus. Please, please be careful. They're extremely dangerous; one bite is agony. Oh, my God." Sniggle and sniffle and *act*. Filthy says this will cause an exit stampede even if the bus has not yet stopped.

Spiders or not, I feel the bite of potential lawsuits against a busline which has been bad to you.

Milk

Speaking of stuff that won't come out or off, according to the Lyndora Moore, condensed milk is a great addition if you want something that (1) won't come off anything, (2) is very messy, slippery and sticky, (3) smells megabad after a few days.

Likewise, Anon writes, "Use Eagle Brand condensed milk as a smelly glue or worse. If this stuff gets a chance to dry, nothing short of sandblasting will remove it."

Sometimes, bad things happen to truly nice people. For instance, Orrie Baysinger wrote to tell me, "My kid spilled some milk in the car. It got into the carpet, under the floormat, molding etc. After one week, we had fermentation and impossible stench. No way to clean it up. It was awful and lasted more than a month. Think about it."

We didn't have to think too long. So thanks, and a tip of the mighty milk mug to you, Orrie.

Music

Here is one of the most ambitious and hilarious ideas yet: how to turn a deserving mark's home into a booming speaker cabinet. Bob the Computer Kid needed to get back at some nasty neighbors who lived in a wood-siding exterior/plaster interior house. Here's what he did.

"You drive a 10 or 20 penny nail with a very broad head into the side of the mark's house, choosing the side with the fewest windows, obviously.

"Then, you attach a violin, viola, bass fiddle or piano wire to the nail. I found that lower frequency wires work best. Apply as much tension as possible on the wire, even stake it. Then stroke it with a music wand—cat gut works best."

Bob says the results are tremendous. "Vibrations amplify through the entire house. The structure is just like a speaker cabinet. The windows will rattle, and the wood will hum. My work made enough eerie, low frequency noise to wake up the mark and his family that night. They were terrified.

"What I did was to paint the nail the color of the house, so I got away with it for two weeks before they found the nail. It was great to sneak out and 'play' their house at two or four in the morning, then disappear and observe the panic and, once, even the police."

Bob says these folks moved after that summer. Evil spirits? Nah, Bob's a nice guy.

Office Nastiness

We can thank local real estate czar Frank Domo for this plan. When your mark has to go to a funeral, is ill, or has some legitimate reason for being away from the office, he or she is vulnerable. That's when you call the boss and/or the boss's secretary and say something like, "Hey, where's old (Mark's Name)? I'm here at the ball park, football stadium, hunting camp, topless bar or whatever, and he has the passes. Where is the old devil?"

It would be great if the square person on the other end of the line piously tried to explain the nature of the true problem. You could chortle and launch into the line, "Oh sure, old (Mark) sure knows how to make 'em up. He said his boss was stupid, but even a terminal idiot wouldn't buy a line like that."

Then you say, after a pause, "Ooops, you aren't the boss, are you? Oh, oh," and hang up.

Officer of the Law

Harry Callahan, who used to be a real law enforcement officer, says it's actually very easy to pass yourself off as a cop. He says that fake IDs and badges may easily be bought and displayed.

"Nobody, but nobody, reads anything on these IDs," says Harry. "Thanks to TV, if you look, talk and act like what people think a cop is, they'll believe you are one. It's really easier than it sounds.

"I've used this scam to scare the living hell out of some dubious people who were acting in a very unsuitable manner. It always worked."

I must add that this is also highly illegal, despite it being unlikely you will be unbadged. Go for it.

Oil

If you have a mark whose machinery or vehicular workings need to be lubricated, Bob the Computer Kid suggests you add carborundum powder to the petroleum at the rate of about three ounces per gallon. This will turn the oil mixture into a liquid sandpaper, which is fabulous for destroying engines. It's quite a nasty trick. The powder is available at hobby stores selling supplies for rock collectors; it's used in polishing.

Outdoor Signs

This is elaborate, but funny. Just ask Killroy. Remove the offending highway directional sign and bring it to a place where you can work on it safely. Paint over the existing letters with the same color of paint as the sign's background. Then spell an annoying message about your mark using retro-reflective tape on the original sign. Do it neatly, cautions Killroy. Replace the sign. Your insult of the mark will reflect to hundreds of folks.

Glad to hear from a whole passle of folks who hail from Chainsaw, Pennsylvania. Included in this randy crew are Little D. Flapper, Cranki, Bullette, Taf, Nancy, Mamie, Jewells, Ike, Muffy and Chuckles. Their MO is messing up the advertising signs at drive-in theaters, restaurants, shops and malls. They reword those types of signs which use movable letters.

They turned the ad for the film *RAIDERS OF THE LOST ARK* into "LOAD OF RAT SHIT REEKS," while *TAKE THIS JOB AND SHOVE IT* became "BAKED JIVE SHIT ON TOAST." They raided a deli sign after hours and created a message about the owner's daughter's lack of virtue with certain farm animals. Another drive-in sorty turned *THE FOUR SEASONS* into "FART ON SUES SHOES," while the other feature, *THE EMPIRE STRIKES BACK,* became "SEMI PRICK TEASER."

Paint

Ed Akni, one of our fine scouts, has found a splendid product that removes paint easily, quickly and chemically. It's called Peel Away, and you just brush it on whatever surface you wish to treat, let it dry, then peel away the paint. It lifts up to eighteen coats! The stuff is patented and has been used all over the world. It first became available in the States in 1983. Ask for it at a hardware or paint store. I just bet you can think of dozens of nasty paybacks you can uncover with this stuff.

Parking Lots

College administrators have to be among the dumb beasts in our fields. Of course, it figures. The weakest students in college today are the education majors; then later, those who flunk out of teaching become the administrators. Or at least, that's what my pal Professor Pudenda McCavitt told me.

Anyway, once while he was in college, Captain Kill found that some ego-stained administrators had proclaimed a major part of prime public parking lot as theirs and instructed workers to put up chains to keep out lesser folks, i.e., teachers and students.

But let him tell it. "Each administrator had been given a duplicate key to open the lock. One evening, I simply slipped another lock on the gate adding to the security, as it were. I had to do this only three times before the idea was dropped, along with the chain.

"I figured if the lazy bastards wanted a prime parking spot, let them get here earlier than anyone else!"

Parking Tickets

Carl Cologne hasn't paid a parking ticket in years. When he finds one on his car, he simply drives or walks around searching for an unticketed car sitting in an expired meter spot. You got it. Carl places his ticket on the other car's windscreen, ala an officer. The other guy, not reading the ticket and feeling guilty anyway, puts his check in the envelope and, voila, the ticket gets paid.

Parties

Block parties, an old favorite, are gaining new favor among the affluent suburbs and the singles housing areas. While block parties can be fun, they can also be damned annoying. Filthy McNasty says that most of those parties have to have a municipal permit. You might want to call and cancel the permit the day of the party, or you could cancel the live music, the caterer, etc.

Quick to cover all avenues, Filthy suggests going the other way by being certain that *lots* of supplies arrive. Call every caterer and booze supply house in town and make sure that each delivers tons of refreshments for the folks. If your block is older folks, rent a punk or new wave band for them.

Here's another grand idea. Go to a remote location and call the police. Have a friend in the background either fire several shots or set off a string of five or six firecrackers. Scream hysterically into the phone about shots being fired. Scream the mark's address, fire some more shots, then hang up. Caution: police record all calls.

PA Systems

It's right out of *Porky's* or *Animal House,* but this gag from CW is funny, and I know it will work because I've used it, too. You have a store, bar or office as your mark. This outfit must have a PA system for it to work to maximum effect. But sometimes in the right setting, plain voice power will suffice.

Anyway, you call the mark-place and tell whomever answers that this is an emergency. You plead with them to page Edward Meoff. Obviously, nobody responds to the page. You sound more emergency stricken, and exasperated in saying, "Oh! OK, I know his brother Jack is there, please page him, quickly."

Success depends largely on your histrionic ability.

Pennies

We all know about gluing a penny to the back of a circuit breaker and how dangerous a stunt that is. But do you remember the chap who fried his mark's fish? Here's an easier way to turn your mark's home aquarium into a fish morgue, if the environment is salt water. Simply drop a copper penny into the tank, and within a couple of days, all those expensive fish will be belly up.

Photography

Some nasty feelings were developing between John Houston and an amateur photographer over some embarrassing personal photos. After all his gentle persuasion turned negative, John moved to fix the mark's darkroom for relief. He filed the edge off a penny and put these metallic shavings into the errant photographer's developer solution for color prints. It made mysterious green spots all over the bad guy's pictures, ruining some vacation photos. As John puns, "Lens be friends."

One of my pals from South Africa relates a special use for the family camera. It seems his younger sister was being a real pain in the arse to everyone at a beach party. He borrowed her little Kodak camera and plotted with a pal. They left the party area, and he took a frontal tight medium shot of his friend peeing. Next he took a close up of his friend's member after the guy had done a little fantasizing. Then he put the camera back in his sister's beach bag. The best part is that little sister had borrowed her mommy's camera.

Police

A trickster with access to his state's statewide police computer plugged in the license number of his mark's car along with a warning about the occupants of this stolen vehicle being armed and extremely dangerous escaped felons. Imagine the fun when two nasty and nervous cops jacked the mark, his stuffy wife, and his mother-in-law out of their car at shotgun point right outside the doors of a ritzy country club. It actually happened.

Estiercol Scaife is the kind of fun guy who will listen to the police band on his scanner until he finds something really tasteless and awful—sort of the crimeland version of seeing Daddy and Mommy Reagan in the nude doing weird things with the Tidy Bowl man. Scaife pulls up to the crime scene with a great show of making enemies and memories by asking all the wrong questions, trying to take Instamatic pictures and seeking gross, personal details. He grins a lot, drools and if appropriate, vomits or flashes money, makes gross jokes and insults people.

I forgot to add, Scaife is doing all of this under the frequently mentioned name of the mark. Tip: Use public transportation for this scam and push just enough so as not to get arrested.

Porno

Who says I don't include something for everybody? Here's one the Moral Majority and those other Old Poops from the Right can use to gross out local porno shops. Smear Vaseline or liquid soap on the covers of their nasty magazines. The effect is startling. Use a squeeze bottle to squirt white liquid soap on their doors and windows. This may demoralize the patrons from coming in the shop. Don't thank me, you owe this one to Filthy McNasty. If you still don't get it, think about it.

Pretty Boys

Everyone knows a chap who likes to shampoo and blow dry his hair every day in imitation of Plastic Man of TV anchorman fame, Mr. Cool Incarnate. Stoney Dale relates that these pains can be had, with a lot of fun.

"Most of these dudes use a certain thick, yellow shampoo which resembles honey. You can pour out some of the shampoo and replace it with thinned-down honey," Stoney writes. "Then your mark will *really* be stuck up."

I bet a lot of you lovely ladies would dearly enjoy doing that to some Mr. Beautiful you know all too well. If so, thank Stoney.

Quotes

Why quotes in a book like this? Sometimes, they make great graffiti. Or they are delightful to drop into conversation. As always, quotes I select make a pungent point. Also the folks who uttered these quotes are very special people. Whatever your reason, don't question mine, just enjoy reading this section. You can use these for any purpose you wish.

"Whenever I see the politicians on TV, I think someone has removed the diving board from the gene pool."

—William Escobar

"If you're the suspect, it's important that you project the blame elsewhere—immediately, forcefully and effectively. When in doubt, accuse."

—Jeff Salzman

"He opens his mouth to eject one obscenity after another. It's endlessly and totally uncouth."

—Vanessa

"Where God hath got it together, let no man put it achunder (sic)."

—Duckbutt Hatcher

"When the birds fly at night, the bone marrow is so good to suck out and chew."

—Mr. D from Austin

"Up against the transformers, muthahertz. All hail the power pirates."

—Jimi the Z

"Youth looks ahead. Old age looks back. Middle age looks worried."

—Sandy Kruckvich

"I'm learning to laugh again, but I'm not sure why."

—Mary V. Benson

"Eat my shorts!"

—Kranki Kathy

"When you resign yourself to fate, your resignation is instantly accepted."

—Paul Wilson

"A broken reputation is tougher to piece back together than a shattered mirror or scattered puzzle."

—Doug Ortman

Relatives

Brian G. is a heavy-hitting jokester. Once he had a family with whom he had to get nastily even. During the course of his planning, one of the family's relatives died. As he knew the family, he readily recognized their voices. With a bit of practice, he was able to recall and imitate the voice of the deceased, at which point he began calling the family at odd hours, playing weird music and sound effects in the background, claiming to be calling from the beyond. Acting like their dead relative, he started haranguing them for their evil ways.

Almost everyone has rotten relatives, folks who become an unwanted part of the family through the curse of birth or marriage, accidents over which we have little control. How then do you grind the ID and EGO of these humanoid hairballs into the dirt, as they deserve? CW to the rescue.

"It's simple. When they send cards, letters or other missives, you just send them back," CW suggests. "Mark their mail 'Refused,' 'Addressee Dead,' 'Moved, left no forwarding address,' or something like that. Then drop it back in a mailbox to be returned. You might even get a few rubber stamps printed with those quasi-official notices like the post office uses.

"When and if they anxiously call you, insist they have the wrong number, talk in a foreign dialect, shout obscenities, or just hang up. Refuse to answer the telephone if it rings again."

Religion

There are a lot of people out there who don't believe in God, which is fine as long as they don't make asses of themselves or pests to you about it. In many respects, they are as bad as the Jesus Junkies. Here's one way of paying back these Godless Goons. Go to some church and fill out a guest card in your mark's name. When you hand in the card, mention a large tithe and pleasantly ask the minister and his family to come calling to the mark's house, say next Sunday afternoon. Make sure your mark will be home for lunch and/ or dinner.

According to Shelli of Goroncy, West Virginia, this trick will turn around on the Jesus Junkies. If your mark is a deserving one and is a very religious person, use the same scenario, only attend some truly off-beat cult or goofo-religion. Perform the same stunt in your mark's name.

Perhaps this idea should go in the "Political" category, but because Discordia Dea sent it to me in good faith, I shall abide by the "Religion" section. Basically, she wanted to get back at a bluenosed Bible Banger who was running for office on a God 'n Morality ticket and plastering the city with horrible signs—true pollution. Polite complaints and requests to his headquarters brought scorn, then the candidate really started to attack his critics by invoking heaven's wrath on them in public. It was time to get even.

Dea got the candidate's home telephone number and put it on some printed election stickers she had made on behalf of the candidate. The stickers took the candidate's basic premise a good bit further to the Fruitcake Right than he wanted. Dea also ran Help Wanted ads on his behalf advertising for "paid staffers" and included the home telephone. "Call anytime, I'm always glad to do the Lord's work," the ad said.

The stickers went up not only on public property, but all over private store windows, church and synagogue doors, etc. They were placed in washrooms, lavatory stalls, on condom machines, etc. You can picture the result, I'm sure.

Here's some happy raps from Tor and Snow Dog for use when the Bible Thumpers come hammering on your door. First, tell them to wait a moment, then close and lock your door. See how long they wait. You can come back every five minutes or so and ask them to wait a little longer. Repeat as needed.

If they want to give you a brochure or pamphlet, accept it with grace. Then give them a pamphlet or brochure in return. This is why I keep telling you to save all that horribly gross direct mail porno you usually toss away. Trade it with your callers.

Finally, pretend you are a member of a weird cult and try to convert them. You can allude to animal sacrifice, Bible eating and removal of clothing, which you should do quickly. Invite them to join you.

Robbery

Let's turn your mark into an armed robber. For this we owe a debt to Chuckles the Cop. Find a convenience store where your mark likes to browse the paperback books, magazines, etc. or where he shops for the evening paper, milk, etc. Learn the inside, behind-the-counter telephone number of the store. As soon as your mark goes inside, rush to a very nearby pay telephone—which you've already staked out—and make a telephone call. Here's what you tell the clerk when he or she answers your call.

"This is a robbery. Don't hang up or look startled, just listen to me! My associate is in your store pretending to browse (describe your mark—appearance, clothes, etc.). He has a gun and will blow your head off if you don't give him all the money in your cash register. I'm telling you this so nobody gets hurt. When he comes to the counter, give him all your money or he'll kill you!"

Hopefully, there is a silent alarm in the place and the clerk has already activated it. The other options are equally amusing, according to Chuckles.

Sail Frogs

People who live in areas where there are large numbers of toads constantly encounter specimens that have been run over and flattened out on the street. When they are so flat and dried-up that they can almost be tossed like Frisbees, they are called "sail frogs." They are also fit for mailing in a first-class envelope. One stamp should be all that's needed, but you might use two, just to be safe.

Samaritan

There is some Good Samaritan in many of you. Let's put it to practice. There are a lot of unfortunate people in our world—ex cons, homosexuals with criminal records and alcoholic and druggie derelicts, for example. Wouldn't it be a fine Christian gesture for your mark to convert his nice suburban neighborhood home into a halfway house for these unfortunate creatures? Why don't you help him?

To start things off, you need to spend a few bucks on a legal ad to be placed in your local newspaper announcing your mark's proposal to open a halfway house for prostitutes, heroin addicts, perverts, etc. at your mark's home address. I guarantee this will stir up the neighbors.

As a corollary, you could also have a trusted associate make some selected stops within the mark's neighborhood, posing as a social worker making inquiries about the mark's reputation preparatory to his opening the halfway house.

School

Does your least favorite teacher put everyone into terminal boredom with slide show after slide show—often really an excuse not to teach? Perk up the action by sneaking a few hardcore porno slides in with the regular ones.

Likewise, Mr. D. has one that some folks from LBJ High School in Austin will remember. It's safe, but fun. Here's how he did it. Take a piece of chalk and carefully bore a hole in one end, making the hole large enough and deep enough to hold a strike-anywhere kitchen match head. Cut the head off a match and fit it into the hole so that only a tiny fraction of the tip protrudes. Glue some chalk powder around the tip to camouflage your work, but leave a tiny bit of match head exposed for striking. Plant it in a classroom.

When used on a chalkboard, the chalk will make a sizzling sound upon ignition of the hidden match head and will spew out a dark column of smoke for several seconds.

I was the epitome of the class clown when I was in high school several hundred years ago. That's no brag, just fact. Here are a few fun things you can do if you're still sentenced there and want to get back at some dictatorial administrators, bumbling bureaucrats or tenuous teachers:

• Draw or paste something very gross or very obscene on pull-down maps, movie screens, etc.

• Take down a roll-up map and screen, lay them flat, then load lime or other dusty substances in them. Carefully roll them back into the holder, then replace them, so that when the mark rolls them back down . . . cough, cough.

• If your school has gone back to the nineteenth century and instituted a dress code to please your own local version of the Rev. Pious Q. Preacher, get as many of your friends as possible to disrupt it without violating it. I bet, for example, it says nothing in there about dying your hair green, picking your nose at lunch, painting your face or vomiting in class.

• Institute massive searches for "lost" contact lenses during assemblies, at lunch, study halls or between classes. Clutter the room and halls.

• Free all the captured animals and insects being held prisoner in the biology labs.

• Send irregular streams of your associates to the office to have some bizarre rumor confirmed or denied.

• As a citizen, demand to see your own school records. Almost everyone else has access to them, so should you.

• If the student newspaper can't or won't do it, publish the salaries of all teachers and administrators. If they are paid with public funds, this information is in the public domain. Demand this data from some uptight bureaucrat in the central office.

• Add some very kinky personal items to selected teachers' mailboxes.

• Create some sort of revolutionary manifesto and leave it around so that it is sure to be discovered. Or have a mole plant it for the administration's gestapo. Then leave cryptic messages about Monday being "D-Day" or X-Day or whatever. The forces of tyranny will be all massed for the revolution that never arrives. It makes them look more like fools.

• Print false notices using official paper and format, then put them in mailboxes. Use your imagination.

• Need forms to copy, examples of the signatures of administrators and teachers? Check office wastebaskets; they are great sources for these bits of valuable raw materials.

• If your school doesn't have a teacher evaluation program by students, make your own. Create forms and pass them out to students. If the bad guys fight you, create nasty publicity and scream about your First Amendment rights.

• Use official channels to announce a going-away party for a teacher who isn't leaving, or a baby or wedding shower for a teacher who shouldn't be or isn't.

Security

So that no bad person will steal your mark's automobile, RV, bike or other vehicle, perhaps you had better secure it. Chain and lock the vehicle to something solid and immovable. If it's dark, the mark may not see the security chain and try to drive off. Can you hear the sound of your security damaging the vehicle? What sweet music.

Sexual Insecurity

Once upon a time, according to Boy Jorges, there was this teacher who was very insecure about his own sexuality. Sometimes, he took this out on his students by being an especially nasty prick. A couple of bright young guys noted this and decided to have some phone phun.

"We called him anonymously and started telling him just how very, very much we thought of him," Jorges related. "Then my pal started getting clinically personal with his compliments. The poor mark got really upset and stuttered all over the place."

According to friends, the mark stewed and worried about this for days, dreading that he was unknowingly sending out gay signals. The two straight tricksters then started putting gay literature into his mailbox and sending him mash notes. After a couple weeks, they tired of all the fun, while the mark continued to worry.

Shut-ins

In honor of Rosey Rosewell, I'd like to dedicate this to people who should never leave home. If you have a mark you hate and wish to isolate at home, fill up your caulking gun with a tube of Liquid Nail. When you know the mark-family is in the house for the evening, loiter outside until all is quiet, then simply place a bead of Liquid Nail to the cracks between door and frame, plus windows and frame.

Ever hear of anyone being locked *in* at home? This stunt is an absolute surprise to the mark. It's also a lot of fun.

Smokers

One of my worst enemies is someone who violates my privacy with his or her smoking in a location or under circumstance where my rights overshadow theirs. Sorry, smokers, I abhor the noxious odor of tobacco smoke. It's too bad your olefactory senses are so far gone you can't smell your own hair, clothes, skin, breath, home, etc. But, I digress.

CW offers a very good trick I have used and used and used. Here's all you do to help a smoker quit—at least in your territory. Add three or four horsehairs to her/his cigarette or cigar. Some disturbed smokers I tried this trick on noticed the smell, others noticed the taste, and happily, two got physically sick.

Soap

Drill a hollow area out of a soap bar, saving the shavings as you go. Fill this hole with the horrible ingredients of your choice. Blood-red ink is an excellent filling. So are smelly substances such as "liver of sulfur" (ammonium sulfide), tuna fish, roaches, beetles and excrement, to name a few.

After filling the cavity, plug the hole with a paste made by mixing the leftover shavings with water. This plug may take a few days to dry. Finally, plant this special bar of soap in your mark's bathroom.

Did you ever try putting a small sliver of soap about the size of your thumbnail into a coffee machine? You will produce an epidemic of Hershey Squirts the likes of which can empty an office in no short amount of time. According to our expert, liquid hand soap will work as well. Oh, boy, where have you gone, Joe DiMaggio?

Sources

This listing is a collection of my findings, plus the suggestions of readers and talk show contributors. Keep in mind that just because these folks are listed here doesn't mean they subscribe to any of the uses to which you'll put their products. Be cool, pay for what you get, but think before you order.

Adam & Even, P.O. Box 800, Carrboro, NC 27510.
    Sellers of everything from adult films and products to X-rated customer film processing and sex aids.

All About Telephones. Tap Books, Blue Ridge Summit, PA 17214.
    This splendid book is cheap and tells you everything technical you need to know about various telephone systems.

Blackhawk, Rt. 1, Box 221, Blue River, WI 53518
    They sell chemicals by mail.

Chemtek, Box 573, Hawkesbury, Ontario, Canada K6A 1X2.
    They sell hard to get chemicals and are very safe, nice people to do business with. They

publish a $2 catalog or you can write with
your needs.

Church of the Tree of Life, 405 Columbus Avenue,
San Francisco, CA 94133.
These folks are very open. Join their church;
among their sacraments is Yohimbine HC1.
(See Drugs.)

**Consumertronics Co., P.O. Box 537, Alamogordo,
NM 88310.**
Here's an active ally in our battle for consumer and human rights. John J. Williams
and his company sells all sorts of publica-
tions, plans and items to arm the foot soldier
in our war against the Big Bad guys. Safe,
sane, confidential service.

Freedom Press, Box 6272, South Bend, IN 46660.
These folks offer a complete book with formulae and instructions for making your own
nitrocyclerine, TNT, C-4, napalm, thermite,
etc. It's written in layman's terms by a real
chemist.

How To Be Your Own Lawyer by Walter L.
Kantrowitz and Howard Eisenberg. NY: G. P.
Putnam, 1979.
This pragmatic book should be in every
trickster's library. Not only might you need
the real advice someday, there is some excellent research in here if you need to use
some legal muscle, too.

Howelab, Box 73, Folly Beach, SC 29439.
> They offer a comprehensive inventory of explosives, fireworks, formulae and instructions for contact/impact grenades, explosive paint, smokescreens, etc.

ITC., INC. Box M508, Hoboken, NJ 07030.
> Here's the place to buy insulting stickers and official looking labels for mailers, letterheads and envelopes.

Juron Company, 3211 W. Rohmann, Peoria, IL 61604.
> These folks sell straitjackets and other law enforcement and institutional restraints.

King's, 21 West 19th Street, New York, NY 11011.
> A true repository of fun, these folks sell decals, stickers, license plates and other good items. If you want to label someone with quality stickers, decals, plates, this outfit will have it. Their specialty is flags and coats of arms from all over the world.

Light, Gene, *Letterheads to Make Your Point.* NY: Harmony Books, 1983.
> This is a useful collection of camera-ready sample letterhead designs to handle various situations.

Merrell Scientific Division, 1665 Buffalo Road, Rochester, NY 14624.
> "We have a complete line of chemicals and signs, everything under the sun."

PW, Rt. 2, Box 125A, Prudenville, MI 48651.
They sell custom bumper stickers for just $2 each. "We'll print any message." No minimum order.

Sample, John. *Methods of Disguise*. Port Townsend: Loompanics, 1984.
This exciting book details how you can disguise yourself—everything from a quickie to a long-term and even permanent change. Lots of examples, illustrations and details. Available from one of the best genre publishers. Loompanics, P.O. Box 1197, Port Townsend, WA 98368.

SME, P.O. Box 251, Warren, OH 44482.
They offer dynamite fuse and electric squibs (igniters). Send them a SASE, and they'll send you a complete catalog.

Southeastern Outdoor Supplies, Inc., Rt. 3, Box 503, Bassett, VA 24055.
They sell Nature's Way Super Skunk Scent. This is the very best because it is a natural scent, and it comes in a spray-on applicator.

Student Science Service, 622 W. Colorado St., Glendale, CA 91204.
According to top agent Laser Davidovich, this outfit is a primo source of chemicals and supplies, including hard to get goodies. Their catalog is $3 by mail.

Tap. Room 603, 147 West 42nd Street, New York, NY 11036.

Subscribe to *Tap,* the phreakers and technological guerrilla war brigade's own publication. If you want reprints or information, send them some money and a SASE, please.

Timberwolf Cutlery, P.O. Box 757, Clanton, AL 35045.

They have a variety of camping, sporting, survival and cutting equipment for mail-order sale.

Sperm Bank

I bet you know some righteous hypocrite who spouts Biblical stuff and criticizes others for nasty things, but who also leads a secret life that's kinky and lewd. Ask any honest hooker who her worst johns are, and she'll always finger some publicly righteous prude who turns into Mr. Hyde for his sexual repression. Let Saucy Sybil suggest some fun for this jerk.

Send a registered letter in the mark's name to the nearest local sperm bank "applying for a loan." Make the letter as straight and naive sounding as possible. Ask that the reply be sent to the home address in strict confidence as the mark admits to an embarrassing sexual dysfunction. It's not as important that you ever discover how or what they responded to the mark. Be happy in knowing that his letter and admission will create all sorts of jokes and silly gossip among the sperm bank's employees. Fun, ain't it?

Spooks

Here's some real inside stuff from Spookland. The CIA is still paranoid about Shasha, the best-yet ID of the KGB mole who is inside. It might be fun suggests our company conner, Laser Davidovich, to make up a stencil which proclaims that Bill Colby (or Dick Helms, Bill Casey, George Bush, or even Ronald Reagan) is Shasha and spray that message all over Washington and environs, including greater downtown Langley.

Here's another idea for spearing the spooks. An accomplice might monitor the employee car traffic from Langley HQ someday, noting where some of the folks go. As most of these people are clerks and analysts without Farm training, this should be easy. You can use your stencil device (above), or use the old bumper-sticker trick. The main thing is that the mark will have to report this matter to CIA security, which will open an investigation and a file.

This idea is universal, i.e., you can do the same thing for embassy employees of your least favorite countries. Of course, the messages will differ, but the results will be the same. Professional paranoia is such a wonderfully universal language.

Spoons

Want to have some harmless fun harassing your mark at the airport? Bob the Computer Kid leads the way. You slip an ordinary teaspoon into the pocket of his three-piece suit while he's at the airport lounge or cafeteria. Imagine the fun on his or her second or third time through the metal detector then having to empty his pockets.

A spoon? People will look and chortle.

Caution, warns Bob. Don't use a knife or fork. They are "weapons" to the humorless people in airport security; a spoon is just clean fun.

Spouses

Maria Mollusk called one of my talk shows with a grand scheme for your mark on the occasion of a party in honor of the happy couple's anniversary. I'll share it with you.

"You go to a selected bar, restaurant or gas station bathroom and remove the seedy, old, cruddy toilet seat from its moorings. Wrap it in a very fancy fashion with a big bow and nice card. The card is, of course, signed in your best forgery of the mark's handwriting or that of his secretary, if appropriate.

"The card says something sweet like 'To my wife (husband) on this special day in honor and loving recognition of the years of . . . (and so on and on,'" Maria explains, chuckling through her beard.

In all probability, denial will be fairly useless in this situation, and the other guests will be either amused or mortified. It will probably end the celebration party, too.

You have an unfaithful spouse or you have a friend who's being cheated on. Sharon the Dismemberment Queen has a civilized way to let lots of folks in on the fun, especially if the cheaters are already married to others.

   "I obtain a typical portrait of the mark, which isn't very hard to do, then I write a brief wedding or engagement announcement in the style of the local newspaper for that area," Sharon explains.

   "My hook is that I use the name, vital stats, etc. of the mark's lover as the other person in the story. True's true, right?

   "Which hurts more, the pain or the fun?" Sharon asks, "happy co-respondent."

Stench

Perhaps this should be filed under fish, but, in honor of the out-of-work jokesters who fished Mellon Bank, here goes. Get the largest fish possible, and after you've removed the hubcap from your mark's car, stuff the fish into the cavity, then replace the cap.

Later, if you can gain access to the mark's air conditioner, remove that cover and place the fish into the impeller while the unit is off. When the unit is turned on, the result is usually spectacular, especially if the fish is aged for a day or so.

Harry Callahan adds, "I once saw a luncheonette closed for a month after this stunt was pulled there. This would also work well in an office or a motel."

If you've ever been gassed you'll enjoy this. After all, there's nothing like military gas training, being Maced or nailed by one of Uncle Gerald's missiles of flatulence. Why not pick your favorite scent, e.g., Mace, CS, etc., and spray a massive load of it into your mark's air conditioning unit intake? Perhaps you could rig such a surprise for the central air conditioning unit intake of a large building that you wish to evacuate, e.g., a club, bar, restaurant, school, etc.

Thanks to Foulbowels Anderson, we now have a splendid payback for someone who is forced to work in a laboratory or other space in which there is not a lot of fresh air, yet there is a commode. Actually, it will work effectively in any sort of closed area where your mark is trapped by work or other circumstance. Let Foulbowels tell his story.

"I had this idiot lab tech I needed to bother. So I came into work early after two straight evenings of drinking beer—lots of it—and eating hardboiled eggs, cheese and blind robins. My flatulence alone was melting structural steel that day.

"I let myself into the tech's small lab about an hour before anyone else was due in the building and turned off the water supply to his commode. Then, I Loctited the water supply handle at the base. I flushed the thing, so now there's no water in the tank. Next, I took one of my most world-class, obnoxious dumps of all time in the tech's commode. That thing was against all the laws of man, nature and civilized warfare. Finally, I cleaned me up, shut the lid down and walked out, closing his door behind me."

Foulbowels says a plumber spent three hours getting things back together—after a one hour wait for him to arrive. In the meantime, the lab tech had no choice but to work in the stench as important tests were due, and the company could not afford for the lab to be shut down. The lab tech had to be sent home in the early afternoon suffering from blurred vision and headache.

Stereos

Have an enemy whose stereo, TV or radio bothers you? Pack some steel wool in the electronic circuits of the offending machine. When the power goes on, the entire board shorts off. Pooooofff. Thanks, Killroy.

Here is yet another idea to discourage inconsiderate louts who play loud stereo music when you need peace and quiet. Much as I like Rock music, I sometimes think New Wave was invented to encourage the practice of audiophonic revenge. In this instance, CW has a grand suggestion if you have ready access to your mark's stereo.

"Replace his good needle with an awful one, an old one, one with a tip like a square nail," CW writes from his redoubt. "Your sabotage-needle will screech, scratch and make all sorts of nasty noise and damage on the records."

How many of you have had to share automobile space with some spaced out cuckoo who plays his in-car system loud enough to shake the moon? Our old pal Col. R. Micheals finally tired of this cacophonous car pooling and created a fireworks display to end all displays.

He literally had come down with migraine headaches from traveling in this vehicular stereophonic sonic boom, but he needed his job so he had no choice, but to Get Even.

"I purchased fifteen feet of dual filament speaker wire and borrowed a couple of Instamatic flash bars. I carefuly spliced the bulbs into the speaker wire in parallel. Since I had access to the guy's car I was able to splice my loaded wire right into his speaker wire system and placed the bulbs all around the inside of his car.

"As they went off in sequence, I was literally able to blow his mind in any direction I chose. As the bulbs exploded, it was like being in an indoor fireworks display. I pretended to be screaming and kicking in panic, too, as part of my cover.

"It cured the problem for as long as I had to ride with the guy. He was so shaken he never did get anything checked or repaired. Nor did he ever turn on the damn machine again."

Store Mannequins

As noted in the Bathroom section, these plaster models make great pseudo victims to entrap real victims. You can use fake blood and your ax-murderer's imagination to create a real mess, e.g., a mutilated "corpse" for someone to find. I once did in a drunken friend who needed to be taught a lesson, i.e., stop hitting on everyone else's ladies. After one of his especially comatose drunkathons, I fixed him up in a sexually compromising position with a store mannequin and took some photos. Then, a friend and I arranged the same scene—live—in his living room for the benefit of his family and guests as they came downstairs much later that morning. It's a good thing I'm a nice guy or I would have used a small boy mannequin.

Stupid Drivers

One of our grossest forms of stupid driver is the lazy numbnuts who parks in zones marked Fire Zone, No Parking/Parcel Pickup, Handicapped Parking or something like that at your mall or supermarket. Selwyn Miles has a very gentle reminder for those mindless jellybrains. After unloading his own shopping cart, he returns the empty cart and places it against the offender's right rear fender. Or if he knows this is a repeat offender or someone who is equally obnoxious, i.e., a jerk or jerkette who refuses to move when asked nicely, Selwyn lays his cart on its side behind the fender. That way, the dumb driver either has to move that cart or, hopefully, won't see it and will ruin some finish on the car when pulling out.

Do you have problems with tailgating by land-bound versions of The Blue Angels? Jimi the Z has pumped up a wonderful response, using his fabled smoke generator. He ran a line into the headers from the electric pump and plastic reservoir from an old windshield washer unit. Jimi wired same to a panel switch. His special "Jimi's Mix" for smoke includes one part WD40, one part drain oil, two parts mineral spirits and a dash of D76 film developer. Not only does the smoke effect work well, according to Jimi, but the stink factor is through-the-roof bad.

If you're not as mechanical as Jimi, a great fan in Tampa suggests you merely load a combination of WD 40 and 40 wt. motor oil in one of those squeeze catsup bottles, open your window and fire the stuff out into the slipstream so it will rush back all over the tailgater's windscreen.

But, don't pull up behind Ed Sasquatch and hit him with the high beams of your Detroit monster. Ed mounted a high-powered spotlight in his ride's rear deck aimed right back at the inconsiderate tailgater. Plugged into his car's cigarette lighter, this 300,000 cp baby gives it right back.

Subscriptions

Here's a switch on the monkey warfare of magazines that use those annoying little advertising inserts. You can use the "Give-A-Gift Subscription" cards that are inserted during the holidays to zap two marks, according to Captain Kill.

Write in one mark's name as the recipient and the other mark's name as the giver. Naturally, you check the "Bill Me Later" box. I like sophisticated, literary humor like this.

Supermarkets

If your local supermarket has been rotten to you and just happens to have an in-store security TV camera, Filthy McNasty has some suggestions. Filthy says, "You can suspend a truly gross centerfold from a porno magazine in front of the lens or get some fat woman to moon the thing. I also pretend to steal, then when I'm confronted, I raise royal hell and threaten lawsuits. Sometimes I get free food as a pacifier."

There are rude shoppers who persist in blocking the aisles while they gab with cronies or let their kids run rampant thorugh the market. They obviously need help, so why not give it to them? Add some small, yet very expensive items to their cart, perhaps burying them among the regular purchases. Some caviar would do well, for example. On the other paw, you could remove staples that look necessary, like diapers, aspirin, Tampax, etc. from their carts.

Tor and Snow Dog have a stunt that sounds like fun. Engineer the total disappearance of your mark's shopping cart very near to checkout time. The best dumping ground is to move the offending vehicle to the preparation area that adjoins the produce department in most chain stores. According to our dynamic duo, this stunt has a grand aggravation factor.

Sweeties

There still seem to be nasty folks doing rotten things to more innocent folks. Sometimes, though, a few of the nice folks win. Steve 10-89G from Racine is a fine example.

His ex-fiance was one of those cheating, flirt-bitches so common on TV soaps and, I guess, in real life also. After their break-up, she had some problems with nasty prank calls which Steve had nothing to do with—just as he wanted nothing to do with her anymore. The calls came from new boyfriends and randy nuts whom she had teased.

Yet her family blamed Steve, and her friends threatened him. Her parents even threatened legal action. Our innocent Steve took action. He made a tape recording in his own voice, saying, "There's a bomb in your house set to go off at 1 A.M. Get everyone out, or I'll blow you all to kingdom come in one hour."

He gave the tape to a very trusted friend and instructed him to call her house that night at midnight. At 10:00 that same night, in front of witnesses, Steve boarded a four-hour flight to Las Vegas to visit his sister, who met him at the airport with witnesses. When Steve's pal played the tape, Steve was over Wyoming talking to some witnesses—a perfect alibi.

Naturally, the police were called and a great and grand furor arose. Steve and his family were indignant—his parents more so because they knew nothing of this scam. Steve and his family threatened legal action against her folks and the police. They refused to even discuss this matter with the ex-fiance or her parents, even when the other folks tried to eat crow, and she called him crying for forgiveness. Great job, Steve!

You probably bought nice, pretty flowers for your sweetie when the going was great. With things as dead as they usually are with ex-sweeties, why not send some bouquets of dead flowers or one with horrible odors, poisons, etc. It's the thought that counts. We thank the IFC Poster Child for this thought.

K. Williams used the mail and some interesting postcards to get revenge on a cad who'd done some nasty things to nice folks. Here's how. "Get a postcard or two from a motel or hotel in a nearby city. Send it to the mark at his home address, or at work if you think it would do more good. Hopefully, his wife, boss or secretary will see it first. You know the mail delivery person will also see it, which can add to the gossip if it's a small town. You can be certain that the wife, boss or secretary will want to discuss this secret life with the mark." Here's a suggested message for the card.

I had a wonderful time the other afternoon (evening), darling. Wow, I had no idea you were such a lover, considering that frump you said you had at home. I just love your tongue and those kinky toys, the video tapes and, well, your, ahh, you know. Sweetheart, I can't wait until the next time. I'll call soon and tell you some things I want you to do with me. See you next week.

Love,

Diane (or whomever)

Of course, with some modification this will easily work on a female mark, as well.

When the Labor Lady from Denver decided to get back at her ex-husband for his myriad extramarital meanderings, she scammed the names and addresses of his many ex-girlfriends—mostly one-week or one-night stands. On Father's Day, she had her teenage kids, with great senses of humor themselves, send mushy cards to Dad in care of each of the girls. In all cases, she noted, the girls dutifully forwarded the cards to dear old Dad. Dad was not amused, she reported.

Let's say your lady has decided to "bed 'em and spread 'em" with another guy, which is her gendered prerogative, of course. You have many options, one of which involves a dildo. You take an especially large, gross model and wire it to hang from the rear license plate holder of her car. Or instead of dangling it down, you can wire it upright or horizontally like a trophy. You might consider different colored dildos, too.

According to A. H. Sylvester, the designer of this devilish dildo delight, it will be days, even a week if you're lucky, before the ex-sweetie discovers why all sorts of folks are staring and laughing at her. Then, she'll know she's been had yet one other way. In addition to women, I bet this could also be used with comically devastating results upon the ego and/or reputation of a gay sweetie.

It's Cara Savage again, back with some devious devilment from our darling damsel. In this scenario, your mark is one or both members of a couple loving, but not living together. Go to your local free clinic and pick up a pamphlet on facts about gonorrhea or some other such social horror story. The bigger the type the better. Carla says to buy some little bitty white envelopes, the same type the clinic uses to dispense pills. Or boost a few of theirs.

"Fill out the front of the envelope with the name of the mark whose apartment or house will be planted," Carla instructs. "When you include the date, back date for five or six days so you imply that the partner is not only infectious, but also cretinous. Then, scrawl in doctorlike writing 1 cap 4x daily, Ampicillan 350."

Carla says to fill the envelope with large, opaque placebo pills and plant it and the literature where a guest is likely to spot them before the host or hostess does. Paranoia and tempers will rage as you have pricked the two biggest social biggies—disease and infidelity.

I first picked this next one up during a telephone talk show in Ohio, but later I saw it in *Playboy*. Basically, a man wanted to end his relationship with his live-in lady. He was leaving on a business trip and told her he would be back in two days and wanted her and her things out when he returned home.

When he got back, he saw that the apartment was in good order and that the girl and her goods were gone. He did notice the telephone was off its cradle, though. Picking it up, he heard a strange language on the line. It turns out the girl had dialed the time and temperature number in Bangkok, Thailand, then left the apartment with the phone off the hook. In *Playboy,* the girl had called Tokyo, and the man's bill was $8,000. Just imagine the hassle with the telephone company, as in "Sorry, but somebody's got to pay." Guess who?

Syringes

As mentioned before, these can be used to inject all sorts of additives into all sorts of products, foodstuffs, containers, etc. James Q. Carter once had an acquaintance in college who kept mooching food from him. After James Q. couldn't make the moocher understand in a civilized way, he injected dish soap into fruit-filled cookies and donuts. After a long stint in the can, the prolific pilferer persisted no more.

Tailgaters

Barney Vincelette, the wily conductor of our symphony of skullduggery, waves his baton at tailgaters, offering them a cacophonous coda. Barney says to hook a cheap, surplus cargo parachute to the rear deck of your car, the luggage rack, or the back of your station wagon or truck. The risers should be secured with rope having a break point of 100 pounds. When the tailgater offends you to your breaking point, inflate the chute so the risers break free and the unit wraps itself around the offending vehicle. Speaking of impaired vision. . . .

Taverns

There was this really big rip-off bar called RandyPants, kind of a rowdy swingers' place. For reasons best left unexplained at this time, Annie Fellantori thought it would be a blast both to get even and to make some money.

"I got a friend to go in on a very crowded, very busy night. He sat right by the door, out of sight of the bar, and collected a buck 'cover charge' from everyone who entered.

"He had a little penlight to make a show of checking IDs, and he used a Magic Marker to make an X on the peoples' hands when they paid. In twenty minutes, he made $108. He split after twenty minutes before some employee got suspicious. I highly recommend this stunt to anyone."

Tea

Like many other druggies, tea drinkers have to get their daily fix of the narcotic caffeine. If your mark happens to be one of those unfortunate addicts, Gnarly Bumpo of Carlsbad Caverns is pleased to offer some very useful advice.

"What's so great about the new packaging of chewing tobacco is that it comes in containers that look just like tea bags. You can probably slip one into some old coot's teacup so he'll make 'baccy' tea. He'll take his first sip and keel over."

Straight shooting there, Gnarly. As a refinement to the idea, you could also switch substances inside those real tea bags or insert additives. Many such custom blends come easily to my twisted mind.

Tear Gas

Mr. Anon suggests that this stuff is, in his words, "dreadfully easy to make." All you have to do is to bubble chlorine gas through acetone in bright sunlight. The sun's ultraviolet light is the catalyst. According to Anon, the resulting chloroacetone is far more effective than commercial tear gas.

Telephones

Is it my imagination, or is it true that since her divorce, Ma Bell has become one of the cheapest, but most costly whores in town? After seeing the high-priced novel that passes as my phone bill, I swear that the Reaganistas and Ma Bell have ganged up to rape us poor folk.

Using a bit of American ingenuity and the reorganization of Ma Bell, you can defeat those locked telephones in offices and other places. Simply unplug the modular cord of the "locked" phone and plug in your own carry-along phone that you probably bought somewhere for ten bucks. Use your phone to make your call on someone else's line and bill. Thank Mike the Madman for this budget easer.

Telephone solicitors are reaching out and touching far too many people, if all the complaints reaching the PUC are an indication of this incursion into our privacy. As usual, most of our flak is directed at the frontline troops—the solicitors. It's true that many of the solicitors are folks just like us—simply trying to make ends meet in these rough times. Most of them will accept a simple "No, thank you." Then there are the rude ones, the others for whom we've reserved the following ideas:

• Ask a few questions about the product or service for sale, then start asking very strange personal questions about the solicitor. Get kinky.

• Listen to the pitch for awhile. Then if the solicitor indicates that he can take credit cards, agree to buy. About halfway through giving your credit card number abruptly hang up. When he calls right back, act totally surprised and pretend total ignorance of what the solicitor is talking about. Either say no and hang up, just hang up or, if you're really devious, start the whole thing over again with the agreement to buy, read half of the card number, etc.

• Blatantly proposition the caller. If he or she is of the same sex so much the better, as it will get him or her off your line quicker.

• Belch, fart or make odd noises into the telephone.

• Begin talking in tongues or start praying.

• Read Allen Ginsberg's poem *Howl* to the solicitor.

Need the name and address of someone and can't get it anywhere? Let Ma Bell help you. Despite the clever conspiracy by Ma and the Reaganistas to split Ma's responsibilities, thus raising her revenues, she still has a department known as CN/A, or Customer Name/Address. CN/A exists so authorized telephone company employees can get the name and address of any customer in any Bell system. All telephone numbers, including the unpublished ones, are maintained on file there.

You use CN/A by acting as a bored, casual employee and call in with a rap something like this: "Morning, this is Bill with Customer Service in Niwot. I've got an old guy on hold who's raising cain about not making a series of calls to area code (303) 555-1212. I need the customer's name for that number." You can also run this backwards, i.e., give the name, get the number. Just act cheery and natural. You can get a list of CN/A numbers in your area from TAP. (See Sources.)

Back from his latest antihitchhiker sortie, Ray Domino is just about to head off for his other job as manager of a church league softball team in Outback, Ohio. But first he says, "This isn't clever, but it makes people sick, so that's good. Snort, sniffle and hawk up some really gross mucous, including greenies and other nasal mucilage, then blow your nose really thoroughly all over the handset of your mark's telephone. It works great in public places."

Want to drive your mark semiserious? According to Anon, many home computers have a telephone autodial capability. For example, the unit on a Commodore Vic 20 can be programmed to dial any number(s) you wish. Set the program in operation and it will go on forever without trace to you. That is, the unit will dial you mark's number, and if the mark answers, your computer will not be satisfied with contact, so, when your mark hangs up, the computer will do it again. Ring that number. Tote that barge. You can program this scam to work forever.

Did you ever want to be a bill collector? It can be a lot of fun, especially if you choose to ignore the 1978 federal law which forbids collection agents from browbeating debtors in a number of situations.

Call your mark late at night at home. Scream and shout, pretend you really hate the mark. Tell him or her you represent some legit company in your city. Be abusive, make strong-arm threats. If you get the spouse, be even more insulting. Call the mark at work. Switch names of collection companies. Spread confusion.

Next, get a trusted friend to do the same thing. Mention real stores that you know the mark frequents. You will soon have the real collection agencies and stores wondering about the mark, who will be calling them, too, trying to track down what's happening. This stunt just seems to snowball. Who knows, maybe you will actually destroy the mark's credit rating for a short while.

Tires

Blasting caps may be hard to get hold of these days. But, if you're as inventive as I am, you might want to really blow a big hole in the tires of your mark's car or whatever. Swab the tire tread with window-cleaner so it's dry and clean. Then use high-quality black electrical or duct tape to fasten two blasting caps side-by-side on the tread of the tire. If you do it right, about two or four revolutions down the road will blow the tire right off the rim. Tape well, sweetie.

Speaking of your mark's tires, always carry a valve wrench so you can remove the valves from his vehicle's tires. This great tool costs under a dollar and is so much safer than a knife or spike when it comes to deflating a tire.

Toilet Paper

According to Stirling Sphincter, bathroom stationery is overlooked when it comes to having fun with people. There are many fine uses, including writing letters on toilet paper, plus this old high school classic.

All you need is a six- to ten-inch piece of toilet paper and some creamy-style peanut butter. Dab some of the peanut butter on the paper and gently pat it in place on the backside of the mark's trousers. It's easily done at parties, for instance, and it may be a lot of minutes before the fun when he discovers your poo poo plant. His protestions upon discovery will serve to make more of an ass of him.

Trappers

I grew up in the country and learned to despise trappers almost as much as land developers and strip miners. Ever see an animal in a trap, dying from trying to chew off its own leg to get loose? I have.

But, let's lighten this up. In fact, let's lighten his load. If you know where one of these cowards is trapping, go along his trap line with some bottles freshly filled (the last couple days) with human urine which you've kept refrigerated. Pour copious amounts on and near his traps. The animals will stay away. If the traps are in the water, spring them with a stick or smash them with a rock. Later, if you get the chance, piss on the trapper personally.

Typewriters

If your mark has one of those typewriters that does not use a ball (the typefaces are on individual keys), Annie Fellantori says you can use needle nose pliers to pry the little typeface heads off the key strikers. Then you simply mix up the letter and replace them, the S on an L key striker, the R on an A, etc.

Universal Price Index

Yet another superhighway on the road to computer domination of our lives is the Universal Price Index, those ugly zebra-stripe lines that now appear on almost all consumer products. They can be had, though.

Mike the Madman points out, "Each pair of lines has a meaning to the encoding device. With the help of a Magic Marker or a black, felt-tip pen you can change that meaning. Just fill in the space between two or more lines, and you screw up the system. Let's show them how much we hate what they are doing to us."

So if a store or a clerk has caused you so much frustration that you want to get back, take a nail or small file and scratch across the magnetic strip or deface the metallic strip on unit pricing products. Your work will either jam the machine or glitch the system.

Utilities

Of course, there is the ultimate. Instead of tampering with, defacing or destroying your mark's electric meter, you could simply steal it. Caution: *Know what you are doing first. Juice kills!* It also entertains. I like this idea because it causes all sorts of problems, both power and bureaucratic. Cut it and run with it. Maybe you could mail or deliver this meter with a ticking death threat to another mark.

Video Games

Want to get even with one of the rip-off artists who manufacture those game cartridges or the shop selling them? According to Jimi the Z, our electronic expert, all they are is two dollars' worth of IC chip in a fifty-cent plastic box, so not much loss there. Jimi says to take a copper marking pen, the type used for PC Board touch ups and run it down the video game cartridge terminal. Blow on it to dry it, and it won't work anymore. You could also do this to your mark's personal cartridge library.

Whistle

I knew there was a reasonable use for a police whistle, and thanks to Bob the Computer Kid, here it is. For some harmless payback to a friend, Bob took a police whistle and, using a heavy-duty, metal-spring tension clamp, mounted it to the underside of his car's front bumper.

"The mount of the whistle must be perpendicular to the plane of the bumper, though," Bob says. "Mount the whistle dead center, and this will produce the rudest sounds possible at speeds of from 5 to 45 miles per hour."

Think of the fun when a mechanic charges your mark twenty bucks to remove the whistle.

Wine

After reading this trick, I'm glad I passed on pressing grapes a few seasons back, if you catch my drift. A fun guy signing himself SOFR says that when a store selling booze really irks him, he goes to the wine area, borrows a couple of jars of the types without seals and takes them to the restroom. He empties out some of the wine and refills the jug with urine from his portable dispenser, then reseals and replaces the product.